I0884497

AMERICA'S STORY

Historical Sources on Colonial Life

CHET'LA SEBREE AND REBECCA STEFOFF

Cavendish Square
New York

Published in 2020 by Cavendish Square Publishing, LLC
243 5th Avenue, Suite 136, New York, NY 10016

First Edition

Library of Congress Cataloging-in-Publication Data

Names: Sebree, Chet'la. | Stefoff, Rebecca.
Title: Historical sources on colonial life / Chet'la Sebree and Rebecca Stefoff.
Description: New York : Cavendish Square, 2020. | Series:
America's story | Includes glossary and index.
Identifiers: ISBN 9781502640772 (pbk.) | ISBN 9781502640789
(library bound) | ISBN 9781502640796 (ebook)
Subjects: LCSH: United States--History--Colonial period, ca. 1600-1775--Juvenile literature. | United States--Social life and customs--To 1775--Juvenile literature.
Classification: LCC E162.S45 2019 | DDC 973.01--dc23

Editorial Director: David McNamara
Copy Editor: Nathan Heidelberger
Associate Art Director: Alan Sliwinski
Designer: Christina Shults
Production Coordinator: Karol Szymczuk
Photo Research: J8 Media

The photographs in this book are used by permission and through the courtesy of:
Cover, 20 Stock Montage/Archive Photos/Getty Images; Throughout book Foxstudio/Shutterstock.com; p. 4 Library of Congress/Wikimedia Commons/File:The Mayflower Compact 1620 cph.3g07155.jpg/CC PD; p. 7, 64 Hulton Archive/Getty Images; p. 8 Kooma/Wikimedia Commons/File:Map of territorial growth 1775.svg/CC PD; p. 14, 48, 69 North Wind Picture Archives/Alamy Stock Photo; p. 16 traveler1116/iStock; p. 25 Francis G. Mayer/Corbis Historical/Getty Images; p. 30 Library of Congress; p. 33 Internet Archive/Wikimedia Commons/File:The white doe; the fate of Virginia Dare; an Indian legend (1901) (14761424616).jpg/CC PD; p. 39 Peter Newark American Pictures/Bridgeman Images; p. 42 Gary Hincks/Science Source; p. 54 Jon C/Wikimedia Commons/File:Triangular trade.svg/CC BY-SA 3.0; p. 56 Print Collector/Hulton Archive/Getty Images; p. 66 MPI/Archive Photos/Getty Images; p. 76 Kean Collection/Archive Photos/Getty Images; p. 80 Universal History Archive/UIG/Getty Images; p. 85, 127 GraphicaArtis/Hulton Archive/Getty Images; p. 88 Museum of Fine Arts, Boston/Wikimedia Commons/File:John Quincy Adams, by John Singleton Copley.jpg/CC PD; p. 90 Historical Society of Pennsylvania/Wikimedia Commons/File:PA-Philadelphia-Penn.jpg/CC PD; p. 94 Stock Montage/Archive Photos/Getty Images; p. 100 Chronicle/Alamy Stock Photo; p. 104, 108, 118 Bettmann/Getty Images; p. 116 Flex/Wikimedia Commons/File:Jonathan Edwards.jpg/CC PD.

Printed in the United States of America

AMERICA'S STORY

CONTENTS

In November 1620, all adult male *Mayflower* passengers signed the Mayflower Compact. By signing this agreement, these men promised to make laws as needed and obey them. The document is a primary source.

Primary Sources

In this book, you will be hearing from many different people from the colonial period in America. The colonial era was a period in which European countries had colonies, or foreign regions under their control, in America. These selections will vary in length. You'll find many easy to understand at first reading, but some may require several readings. All the selections have one thing in common, however. They are primary sources. They are important to us because they are the core material for all historical investigation.

What Is a Primary Source?

The term "primary source" is the name historians give to the information that makes up the record of human existence. A primary source is "history" itself. Primary sources are evidence. They give historians the all-important clues they need to understand the past.

Perhaps you have read a detective story in which the detective must solve a mystery by piecing together bits of evidence he or she uncovers. The detective makes deductions, or educated guesses, based on the evidence, and solves the mystery once all the deductions point in a certain way. Historians work in much the same way. Like detectives, historians analyze the data by careful reading and rereading. After much analysis, historians draw conclusions about an event, a person, or an entire era. Historians may analyze the same evidence and come to different conclusions. This is why there are often disagreements about an event among historians.

Primary sources are also called documents. It is a rather dry word to describe what can be just about anything: an official speech by a government leader, an old map, an act of Congress, a letter, a diary entry, a newspaper article, a song, a poster, a cartoon, a photograph, or someone captured on tape or film.

By examining the following primary sources, you will be taking on the role of historian. Here is your chance to jump into an exciting period of American history. In this book, you'll examine the decades before the American colonies became the independent nation known as the United States. You'll come to know the voices of the men and women who settled an unknown place and built communities. You'll read the words of Native Americans and government officials, servants and slaves, farmers and rebels. All of these documents help us to understand what it was like to live in the era that gave birth to the United States.

How Do You Read a Primary Source?

Each document in this book deals with some aspect of life in colonial North America. The pieces of history quoted come from many different writers with different experiences and levels of education. Several hundred years ago, even educated people used spelling, grammar, and vocabulary words differently than we use them today. The colonial vocabulary also contained words that

Jamestown, Virginia, was the first permanent English settlement in America. Here, settlers cut and carry lumber to build the settlement.

will be unfamiliar to someone living in this century. Don't be discouraged! Trying to figure out language is exactly the kind of work a historian does. Like a historian, you will have a deeper, more meaningful understanding of the past.

As you read each document, ask yourself some basic questions. Who is writing or speaking? Who is that person's audience? What is the writer's point of view? What is he or she trying to tell the audience? Is the message clearly expressed, or is it implied (that is, stated indirectly)? What words does the writer use to convey his or her message? Are the words emotional or objective in tone? These are questions that can help you think critically about a primary source.

There are also some tools in each chapter to help you unpack these documents. Some terms and concepts you may not be familiar with have been explained in sidebars. Also, questions follow each of the documents to help you focus and think through the primary source you have just read. As you read each selection, you'll probably come up with many questions of your own. That's great! The work of a historian always leads to many, many questions. Some can be answered; others cannot and require further investigation.

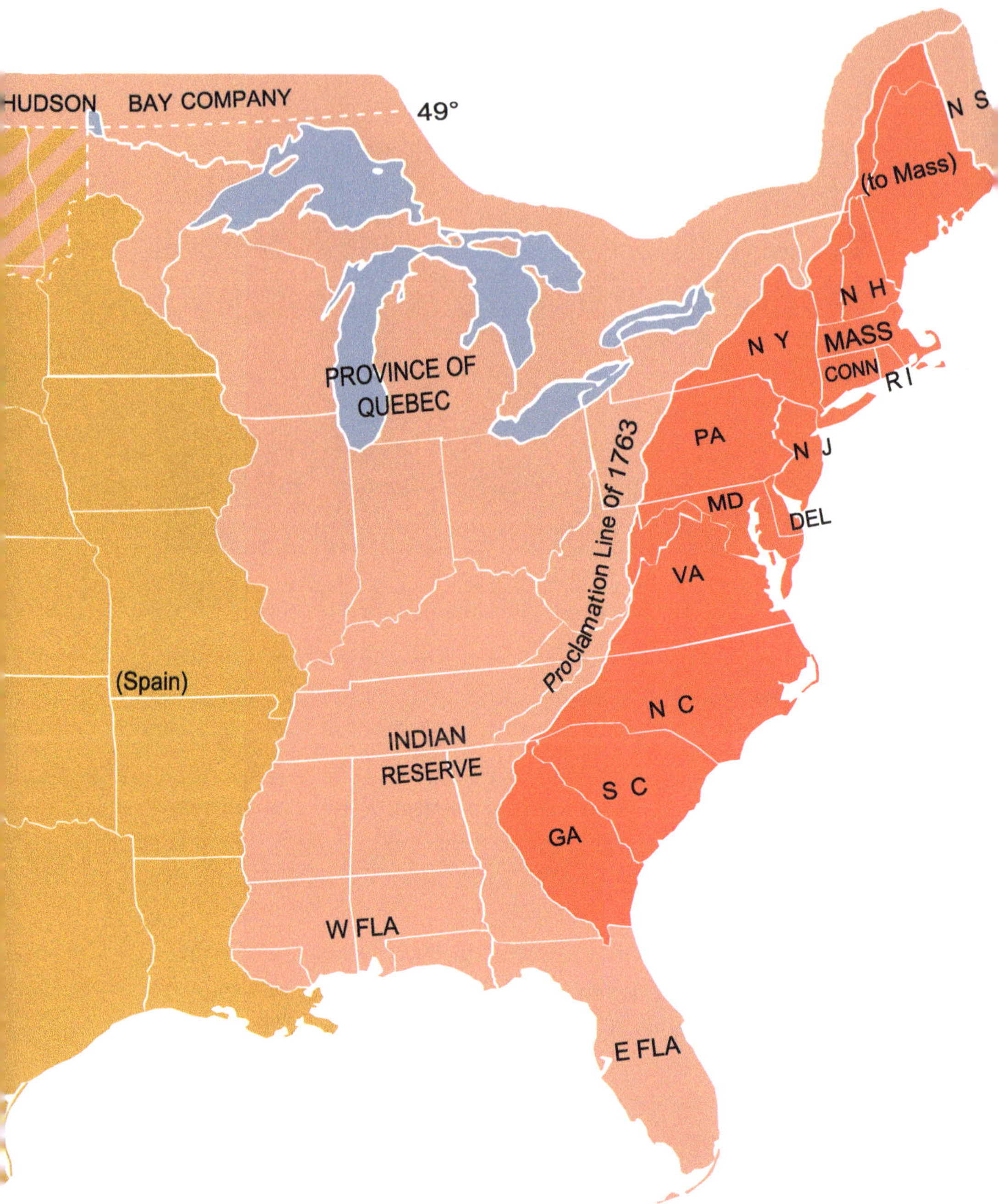

This map shows the division of land after the French and Indian War. France gave all its North American land east of the Mississippi River, including the Province of Quebec, to the British. The land west of the Appalachian Mountains was reserved by the British for Native Americans.

INTRODUCTION

Colonies in the New World

Many people think of the British when they think of colonial America. That make sense since the British colonies and those who rebelled against British rule are responsible for creating the present-day United States. However, colonial America also included many colonial settlements, or newly established communities or towns, from other European nations. In fact, some of those foreign settlements helped shape the two-hundred-year history of British colonial America.

Other Countries' Colonies

Spain was the first European nation to claim an American colony. In 1492, Christopher Columbus led a Spanish expedition across the Atlantic. He was hoping to reach China. Instead, he arrived in the Caribbean. Just a few decades later, the Spanish conquistadors, or conquerors, invaded Mexico. After overthrowing, or forcibly removing, the Native American Aztec civilization, the Spanish established a colony called New Spain.

This colony would eventually control all of Mexico, much of Central America, and part of the present-day United States. By the middle of the sixteenth century, Spain had added what are now Florida, Texas, New Mexico, Arizona, Utah, Nevada, and California to its territory. Most of the Spanish colonies in North America, however, were far from the British ones. For that reason, the British colonists had little to do with them.

The French also had colonies in North America. France sent ships to the mouth of the Saint Lawrence River, which is near the border between eastern Canada and the United States today. France made its first attempt to establish a colony there in 1541. In 1608, however, France established its first lasting settlement, the city of Quebec. The French called their North American territory New France. It grew into a large region around the Saint Lawrence River and the Great Lakes.

British Exploration

Britain's claim to territory in North America was almost as old as Spain's. In 1497, King Henry VII hired a navigator named John Cabot to explore the new lands that Columbus had reported in the western Atlantic. Cabot is believed to have landed somewhere on the east coast of North America, probably in present-day Newfoundland. The English felt that Cabot's voyage gave them a territorial claim. For many years, however, the only English voyagers were fishermen who braved the stormy Atlantic to fish off the North American coast.

England did not become officially interested in North America until the late sixteenth century. At that time, navigators were looking for something that geographers called the Northwest Passage, a sea route that would lead from the Atlantic Ocean to China. Obsessed with finding this passage, England saw North

America as an obstacle, something to sail through or around. During the 1570s and 1580s, English explorers such as Martin Frobisher and John Davis searched the northeastern coast for the passage. They did not find it because it did not exist. They did, however, learn more about America.

The British Colonies

Some English explorers and merchants started thinking about colonies. Colonization would have several advantages. First, settlers in the North American wilderness would have to buy cloth, tools, glass, and other goods from British merchants. Second, the colonists could supply useful raw materials such as wood and furs from new places. Perhaps they would even find gold. Ever since Spain found gold in Mexico, Europeans had dreamed of finding another such source of wealth.

Several groups of English merchants and investors tried to start colonies in North America in the late sixteenth and early seventeenth centuries. During the 1580s, some English settlers founded a small colony on Roanoke Island off the coast of present-day North Carolina. By 1590, however, the colony had disappeared. Historians still do not know what happened to the Roanoke colonists. An early attempt to start a colony in Maine also failed. But in 1607, the English managed to establish a permanent settlement called Jamestown in Virginia. Thirteen years later, a ship called the *Mayflower* brought the first settlers to New England, the name we still give to the northern part of the region that the English colonized.

Two other European nations founded settlements in eastern North America. At the time, the Dutch were building an empire of trade and colonization in Asia. However, they also took an interest in North America, mainly as a source for furs. In 1614, merchants from the Netherlands set up a trading post near present-day Albany, New York. Ten years later, settlers began arriving in the colony that the Dutch called New Netherland, which stretched along the Hudson River. Its main town was New Amsterdam on Manhattan Island. It had an excellent harbor and soon became a busy port.

In 1638, Sweden established a small colony south of New Netherland on the Delaware River. The colony, known as New Sweden, only survived until 1655, when the Dutch captured it and added it to New Netherland. Nine years later, however, the Dutch colony in turn fell to an English fleet sponsored by the Duke of York. New Netherland became the British colony of New York.

By the middle of the eighteenth century, thirteen North American British colonies stretched along the Atlantic coast. They went from the border of New France in the north to the border of Spanish Florida in the south. More than one million people lived in the thirteen colonies by 1760.

Although this population included men and women from many national and ethnic backgrounds, most of the white colonists were from England, Scotland, Ireland, Germany, and the Netherlands. The overwhelming majority of black people, who were enslaved by white colonists, where brought to colonial America from countries in western Africa.

Transatlantic Tensions

Although an ocean separated the colonies from their parent countries, events in Europe had a powerful impact on colonial life. When Great Britain and Spain went to war in the early eighteenth century, for example, fighting broke out between the Spanish in Florida and the southernmost British settlements. Britain and France were frequently at war during the colonial period. This meant that their colonies were often at odds.

The British and French colonies developed very differently. The British colonies had more settlers and developed an agricultural economy. Additionally, they exported raw materials. Exportation is the sale of crops, goods, or materials to another country. Despite its large size, New France attracted far fewer settlers. Its economy was based almost entirely on trade, mostly of furs. Explorers, trappers, and traders from New France traveled far inland into the heart of the continent. The British, however, were slow to explore beyond the Appalachian Mountains, the western border of their colonies. The French colonists also built stronger relationships with the Native Americans. While the British concentrated on developing their coastal colonies, the French built a network of forts, trading posts, and Native American alliances throughout the Great Lakes region, in the Ohio River valley, and along the Mississippi River. Eventually, the British colonies were almost surrounded by French territories.

The French and Indian War

Fighting between the French and the British broke out in the colonies when British colonists began buying furs and building forts on northern and western frontiers, or lands beyond their colonial boundaries. When France and Great Britain went to war in Europe, their colonists also fought. The colonial period saw a series of such conflicts, which resulted in a long war. In European history, this war is known as the Seven Years' War (1756–1763). The British colonists, however, called it the French and Indian War because it pitted them against the French and their Native American allies. In North America, fighting began in 1754.

Fought largely on the frontier and in the Ohio River valley, the war ended in crushing defeat for New France. British forces captured Quebec and Montreal, the colony's two cities. The Treaty of Paris officially ended the conflict in 1763. A treaty is a formal agreement between two parties. This particular treaty gave France's territory in Canada and the territory east of the Mississippi River to Great Britain.

Now that Great Britain controlled North America all the way to the Mississippi, British colonists were ready to travel across

George Washington fought for the British during the French and Indian War. He is shown here directing his troops.

the Appalachians into the new territory. However, Great Britain passed the Proclamation of 1763 after the war as well. The law declared the colonists could not settle west of the Appalachian Mountains, while Native Americans could not settle east of them. In this way, the British government hoped to avoid further fighting with the Native Americans. Although the Proclamation of 1763 angered colonists who had thought they were fighting for access to the western territories, it was just one source of the frustration that many colonists felt with British rule by the middle of the eighteenth century.

Seeds of a Revolution

Conflicts over tax laws and a growing desire for control over their own government drove the colonists ever closer to a break with Great Britain. In the mid-1770s, their frustrations turned into an armed rebellion that became the American Revolution, or the American War of Independence. It ended the colonial era.

In this book, you will read firsthand accounts of people who lived through this era. Through European explorers and colonists, Native Americans, and enslaved Africans, you will learn about life in the changing landscape of colonial America. This is the beginning of America's story.

Settlements in colonial America required a lot of manual labor, since settlers were gathering materials and building from the ground up.

1 The Birth of the Colonial Era

The first successful British colony was Virginia. It was founded in 1607 by the Virginia Company of London. They received a charter, or written grant, from King James I. The company hoped to find gold as the Spanish had in Mexico. Although they did not find any, they found other goods like tobacco to be profitable, or something they could make money from. Other settlements in search of riches sprung up in northern regions of the New World. However, something other than the search for profitable trade began to draw more settlers to colonial America.

Religious Freedom

Religious differences led to the founding of several settlements. Some members of the Church of England, or the Anglican Church, believed that the church needed to be reformed, or changed. They were called Puritans.

Others, called Separatists, wanted to break away completely. The Separatists found religious freedom in the Netherlands. Some, however, sailed to the New World on the *Mayflower* in 1620. These individuals were known as the Pilgrims. They were called this because they viewed their voyage as a pilgrimage, or a journey with a religious or spiritual purpose. The Pilgrims established the Plymouth colony. Ten years later, a group of Puritans, with a royal charter, established Massachusetts Bay Colony near Plymouth. As Massachusetts grew in population and influence, it absorbed Maine, which never existed as a separate colony. In 1691, it also absorbed Plymouth.

Despite gaining territory, some Massachusetts colonists ended up forming two new colonies in New England because of religious differences. In 1636, Rhode Island and Connecticut were established. Settlers who were unhappy with the Puritan leaders moved to Connecticut to establish their own government. Those who established Rhode Island, however, were actually driven out of Massachusetts because their beliefs began to differ from Puritan ideas.

Maryland was also founded because of religious differences. Lord Baltimore, a Catholic nobleman, established the colony in 1632 as a safe place for Catholics. They were being persecuted, or treated poorly because of their religious beliefs, in England. In Britain, the majority of people were Protestants, or Christians who had separated from the Catholic Church, like those of the Church of England.

Trade, Acquisitions, and Alternatives

Although religion was a large factor in colonial America, many colonies were founded for other reasons. For instance, the establishment of the Carolina colony, much like the establishment of Virginia, was based around potential profits. In 1663, a group of noblemen received permission to establish the Carolina colony.

They were hoping to make money from trade and land sales. In 1729, the colony split into North and South Carolina.

The year after the founding of Carolina, the Duke of York acquired the Dutch and Swedish territories along the Hudson and Delaware Rivers. He renamed the area New York and gave its southern part to two friends, who founded New Jersey.

The Pennsylvania colony was created by a royal charter in 1681. Delaware, the last colony in the Middle Atlantic region, was originally part of New York and then Pennsylvania. It became its own colony in 1704, though it still shared a governor with Pennsylvania.

The last of all of the colonies to be founded was also the southernmost. General James Oglethorpe founded Georgia in 1732. The colony served as a buffer between the British colonies and Spanish Florida. Georgia was also a colony where people who were poor or in debt in England could go to start over.

John Smith Reflects on Jamestown

One member of the expedition to establish a colony in Virginia was a twenty-seven-year-old soldier and adventurer named John Smith. Smith was at odds with the group's leader. For that reason, he had little voice in the colony at first. However, after the ships that had brought the colonists returned to England and supplies ran low, the efficient and practical Smith helped guide Jamestown through a period of hardship. Survivors later called this period the "starving time." The colonists made Smith their governor from September 1608 to September 1609. Then, hounded by complaints and criticism, he returned to England. In 1624, he published *The Generall Historie of Virginia, New England, and the Summer Isles*. The book is a description of British exploration and settlement in the Americas. It contains the following account, written by Smith and three other colonists, of events in Jamestown after the ships departed in June of 1607. They left about one hundred men behind in the new colony.

Captain John Smith was a soldier and sailor who joined the Virginia Company. He helped establish the Jamestown settlement and saved its people from starvation and ruin.

Being thus left to our fortunes, it fortuned that within ten days scarce ten amongst us could either go, or well stand, such extreme weakness and sickness oppressed us. And thereat none need marvel, if they consider the cause and reason, which was this.

Whilst the ships stayed, our allowance was somewhat bettered, by a daily proportion of biscuit, which the sailors would pilfer to sell, give, or exchange with us, for money, sassafras, furs, or love. But when they departed, there remained neither tavern, beer house, nor place of relief, but the common kettle ... [Our President kept the best food and allowed us] half a pint of wheat, and as much barley boiled with water for a man a day, and this having fried some 26 weeks in the ship's hold, contained as many worms as grains; so that we might truly call it rather so much bran than corn, our drink was water, our lodging castles in the air.

With this lodging and diet, our extreme toil in bearing and planting palisdades, so strained and bruised us, and our continual labor in the extremity of the heat had so weakened us, as were cause sufficient to have made us as miserable in our native country, or any other place in the world.

From May, to September, those that escaped, lived upon sturgeon, and sea crabs, fifty in this time we buried, the rest seeing the President's projects to escape these miseries in our pinnace by flight (who all this time had felt neither want nor sickness) so moved our dead spirits, as we deposed him ...

But now was all our provision spent, the sturgeon gone, all helps abandoned, each hour expecting the fury of the savages; when God the patron of all good endeavours, in that desperate extremity so changed the hearts of the savages, that they brought such plenty of their fruits, and provision, as no man wanted.

—Reprinted in John Lankford, ed., *Captain John Smith's America* (New York: Harper & Row, 1967).

CONSIDER THIS

1. What was the leader of the colony planning to do before the settlers got rid of him?
2. How would you describe the planning and leadership of the Jamestown colony in this first year?

A Government for and by the People

The Pilgrims who sailed to North America in 1620 on the *Mayflower* planned to settle north of Jamestown in Virginia. However, they landed much farther north, in what became Massachusetts. They went ashore at a place called Plymouth. It was mapped six years earlier by Captain John Smith of Jamestown.

The *Mayflower* passengers were not a group of people with shared beliefs. Out of the 102 people aboard the ship, less than 40 were Puritans. The rest were craftspeople, laborers, and farmers. Knowing that they would need a way to govern this mixed community, the Pilgrim leaders wrote a compact, or agreement. In it, they promised to make laws as needed and to obey them. All the men—Puritans, craftspeople, laborers, and farmers—signed it. This document is called the Mayflower Compact. It was neither a system of government nor a constitution. However, it sets forth the idea that settlers in the new continent had a right and a responsibility to govern themselves.

> Having undertaken, for the Glory of God and our advancement of the Christian Faith and Honour of our King and Country, a Voyage to plant the First Colony in the Northern Parts of Virginia, do by these presents solemnly and mutually in the presence of God

KEY TERMS AND CONCEPTS

From John Smith's account of Jamestown:

palisdades Palisade, or a defensive fence or wall made from wood.

pilfer To steal.

pinnance A small boat, usually with sails or oars.

savage A term settlers and colonists used for Native Americans.

scare Only.

From the Mayflower Compact:

civic body politic One united governing body.

covenant An agreement.

and one another, Covenant and Combine ourselves together into a Civil Body Politic, for our better ordering and preservation and furtherance of the ends aforesaid; and by virtue hereof to enact, constitute and frame such just and equal Laws, Ordinances, Acts, Constitutions and Offices, from time to time, as shall be thought most meet and convenient for the general good of the Colony, unto which we promise with all due submission and obedience. In witness whereof we have hereunder subscribed our names at Cape Cod, the 11th of November, in the year of the reign of our Soveriegn Lord King James, of England,

France and Ireland the eighteenth, and of Scotland the fifty-fourth. Anno Domini 1620.

—Quoted in Frank R. Donovan, *The Mayflower Compact* (New York: Grosset and Dunlap, 1968).

CONSIDER THIS

1. What did the Pilgrims give as their reasons for coming to North America?
2. According to the compact, what characteristics would the Pilgrims' laws have?

William Penn's "Holy Experiment"

In 1681, King Charles II of England granted William Penn a large amount of land in North America. It was payment of a debt Charles owed to Penn's father. The king named the grant Pennsylvania, which means "Penn's woods" in Latin, in honor of Penn's father. Penn was a Quaker, a member of a Christian religious minority that had been persecuted in the British Isles. Penn declared that his colony would be a "Holy Experiment." It would be a community shaped by the Quaker ideals of peace, equality, and tolerance. It would be open to Christians of all sects, or groups. But Pennsylvania was more than an experiment in the Quaker way.

As proprietor, or owner, of the colony, William Penn expected to make money from the rents and taxes the colonists would pay. He advertised Pennsylvania's virtues and worked hard to attract settlers from several European countries. Penn also hoped that the thousand or so Europeans who were already living in Pennsylvania when he acquired it would stay there. In April 1681, before he arrived in his colony, he sent its residents a letter to introduce himself.

When William Penn arrived in the Pennsylvania colony, he worked to establish a good relationship with the Native Americans living on the land.

My Friends,

I wish you all happiness here and hereafter. These [words] are to let you know that it hath pleased God, in his providence, to cast you within my lot and care. It is a business that, though I never undertook before, yet God hath given me an understanding of my duty, and an honest mind to do it uprightly. I hope you will not be troubled at your change, and the King's choice, for you are now fixed at the mercy of no governor that comes to make his fortune great; you shall be governed by laws of your own making, and live a free, and if you will, a sober and industrious people. I shall not usurp the right of any, or oppress his person. God has furnished me with a better resolution, and has given me His grace to keep it. In short, whatever sober and free men can reasonably desire, for the security and improvement of their own happiness, I shall heartily comply with, and in five months resolve, if it please God, to see you. In the mean time, pray submit to the commands of my deputy, so far as they are consistent with the law, and pay him those dues (that formerly you paid to the order of the Governor of New York) for my use and benefit; and so I wish God to direct you in the way of righteousness, and therein prosper you and your children after you.

I am your true friend,

Wm. Penn

—Quoted in Bonamy Dobrèe, *William Penn: Quaker and Pioneer* (Boston: Houghton Mifflin, 1932).

CONSIDER THIS

1. What virtues or qualities did Penn encourage?
2. How would Penn's colony differ from what settlers had experienced in their homelands?

KEY TERMS AND CONCEPTS

From William Penn's letter:

furnish To give.

prosper To be wealthy or successful.

usurp To forcibly take away.

The Costs of a Colony

After James Oglethorpe founded the Georgia colony in 1732, he asked the British government to repay him for the money he spent in Georgia "for the Preservation and Defence of His Majesty's Dominions on the Continent of North America." In other words, he wanted to be repaid for the money he had spent maintaining the colony. In 1743, Oglethorpe produced a list of expenses, including those shown here.

These are not just boring numbers. Instead, they paint a lively picture of life in early Georgia. The list depicts the everyday business of fixing wheelbarrows, patrolling borders, and trading with the Native Americans. However, it also depicts more exciting elements of colonial life like fires, arrests, and alligator hunts. The symbols at the top right of the list stand for pounds, shillings, and pence, units of British currency at the time. There were twenty shillings in a pound, and twelve pence in a shilling. One pound in 1743 would be equal to about $230 in 2018.

	£	S.	D.
To Captain Hugh Mackay for 10 boatchains, Padlocks, Staples and 45 feet of Chain	5	4	0
To Edward Rush for mending and cleaning 67 Indian guns	1	2	1
To 5 Soldiers for assisting to put out a fire	0	10	0
To Samuel Williams for killing an Allegator	0	5	0
To Thomas Hucks Esqr and William West for 15 Tons of Strong Beer in 8 Barrels with 2 Iron Hoops each	119	8	0
To Thomas Marriott for Pipes and Tobacco for the Indians	0	2	0
To Francis Moore which he paid over to Sergeants Cook and Bailey and some others and to 7 Soldiers being a Gift to them on St. George's Day	2	7	6
To Michael Martin for taking a Deserter [capturing a runaway soldier]	5	0	0
To Mary Matthews for her being Interpreter to the Chiefs of the Creek Indians	20	0	0
For sundry utensils for John Saller's Scout Boat	4	17	1½
For 7 pounds of meats and 7 pounds of bread each week for each of 100 privates, Highland Independent Company, 2 May 1740 to 2 September following	761	10	0
To Thomas Walker in full for a Roof to the Arsenal	10	0	0
To Thomas Loop for mending Wheelbarrows	0	6	0
To John Brownfield for making 27 Shirts for Indians	1	13	9

—Quoted in Webb B. Garrison, *Oglethorpe's Folly: The Birth of Georgia* (Lakemont, GA: Copple House Books, 1982).

CONSIDER THIS

1. Why do you think Oglethorpe paid for shirts, pipes, and other gifts for the Native Americans?
2. Why did Oglethorpe expect the British government to repay his expenses for arming and feeding soldiers?

Colonial America

By the mid-1700s, the thirteen colonies that would one day become the beginnings of the United States had been established. The establishment of these colonies, though, was not without its struggles and hardships. Explores, settlers, and pioneers would encounter new terrains, new cultures, and an altogether new world. Ultimately, they would have a diverse set of reactions to this strange new place.

Martin Waldseemüller made the first map of the world that featured the land mass he named "America." He named it for Amerigo Vespucci, an Italian navigator and explorer.

2 Explorers, Pilgrims, and Pioneers

Western Europeans were not in search of a new world when they first took to the seas. They were in search of new routes to sail for the spice trade, which was the transportation and sale of spices and herbs from Asia. Since the Venetians had control over the eastward routes to Asia, explorers like Christopher Columbus and John Cabot sailed west across the Atlantic Ocean in search of the eastern shores of China. Soon, however, European explorers and geographers realized that the land they encountered was not China.

America: The New World

In 1507, a German mapmaker named Martin Waldseemüller made a map of the world that showed a landmass west of Europe. He labeled that land mass "America." This name was in honor of an Italian navigator, or a person who directs the course of a ship, named Amerigo Vespucci. He had made several voyages across the Atlantic. Other mapmakers began using the name. Before long, the new continents were known as the Americas.

They had another name as well: the New World. Everything in this New World was a surprise. The land, the Native people and their civilizations, and the plants and animals were all foreign to the Europeans. But was the New World a paradise or a frightening wilderness?

Diverse Perspectives

From the earliest days of exploration to the end of the colonial period, people found the New World to be both amazing and terrifying. To some, North America seemed to be filled with plentiful resources and natural marvels. Many felt that God had created it to be settled by Europeans. This belief certainly made it easier for the Europeans to push out the Native Americans.

Some people, however, saw North America as dark and dangerous. They thought it was populated by savage people and fierce beasts such as bears and wolves. These animals were quite rare in the settled parts of Europe. God may have wanted the Europeans to settle in North America, but doing so would be a test of faith that would require strength and courage. In the end, whether people saw the Americas as a challenge or an opportunity, everyone had to find a way to survive and thrive in the New World.

Early Accounts of Native Americans

Giovanni da Verrazzano was one of the first Europeans to see the Atlantic coastline of the future United States. He was an Italian explorer and navigator. King Francis I of France hired Verrazzano to find a route to China via the Atlantic Ocean. In 1524, he arrived near Cape Fear in present-day North Carolina. He explored the coast all the way to Maine. His account of the voyage was widely circulated in sixteenth-century Europe. It contains one of the first detailed descriptions of Native Americans.

> The people are of color russet and not much unlike Saracens; their hair black, thick, and not very long, which they tie together in a knot behind and wear it like a tail. They are well featured in their limbs, of mean stature, and commonly somewhat bigger than we. They are broad breasted, with strong arms. Their legs and other parts of the body are well fashioned and they are disfigured in nothing, saving that they have somewhat broad visages, and not all of them. For we saw many of them well favored, having great and black eyes, with a cheerful and steady look. They are not strong of body, yet sharp witted, nimble, and great runners ... The people go entirely naked except that they cover their privy parts with certain skins of beasts like unto martens. They fasten these onto a narrow girdle made of grass, very artificially wrought, and hanged about with tails of divers other beasts dangling about their bodies down to their knees. Some wear garlands of birds' feathers.
>
> —Quoted in Bill Lawrence, *The Early American Wilderness: As the Explorers Saw It* (New York: Paragon House Publishers, 1991).

This is an image of Manteo, the chief of the Croatan tribe. The Croatan people lived near present-day North Carolina.

CONSIDER THIS

1. Does Verrazzano's description contain any clues about his opinion of the Native Americans he saw?

A Pilgrim's Fear of the New World

Nearly a century after Verrazzano's voyage, the *Mayflower* arrived in present-day Cape Cod, Massachusetts. William Bradford, who was governor of Plymouth for many years, later wrote a history of Plymouth's founding and early years. After being passed down within the Bradford family for generations, this manuscript was placed in a Boston church. During the American Revolution, the British seized it and carried it off to London. The account was not discovered and published until 1856. It describes the Pilgrims' feelings in the early days of the Plymouth colony.

> Being thus passed the vast ocean, and a sea of troubles before in their preparation ... they had now no friends to wellcome them, nor inns to entertaine or refresh their weatherbeaten bodys, no houses or much less townes to repair too, to seek for succoure ... And for the season it was winter, and they that know the winters of that countrie know them to be sharp and violent, and subjecte to cruell and feirce stormes, deangerous to travill to known places, much more to serch an unknown coast. Besids, what could they see but a hidious and desolate wildernes, full of wild beasts and willd men? And what multituds ther might be of them they knew not ... [W]hich way soever they turnd their eys (save upward to the heavens) they could have little solace or content in respecte of any outward objects. For summer being done, all

KEY TERMS AND CONCEPTS

From Giovanni da Verrazzano's account:
artificially wrought Artfully or cleverly created.
Saracen An old European term for a Muslim or Arab.
visage Face.

From William Bardford's manuscript:
adversitie Adversity, such as a difficulty or misfortune.
civill Civilized.
hiew Hue or appearance.
maine barr Main barrier.
succoure Succor, or assistance and support during difficult times.

things stand upon them with a wetherbeaten face; and the whole countrie, full of woods and thickets, represented a wild and savage hiew. If they looked behind them, ther was the mighty ocean which they had passed, and was now as a maine barr and goulfe to separate them from all the civill parts of the world … What could now sustaine them but the spirite of God and his grace? May not and ought not the children of these fathers rightly say: Our fathers were Englishmen which came over this great ocean, and were ready to perish in this wildernes, but they cried unto the Lord, and he heard their voyce, and looked on their adversitie, etc.

—Reprinted in William T. Davis, ed., *Bradford's History of Plymouth Plantation: 1606–1646* (New York: Charles Scribner's Sons, 1908).

CONSIDER THIS

1. How would you describe Bradford's overall reaction to his first glimpse of the New World? Why do you think he felt that way?
2. As the Pilgrims faced the New World, what did Bradford see as their great support?

A Pilgrim's Praise of the New World

In 1652, Native Americans of the Mohawk tribe kidnapped sixteen-year-old Pierre Esprit Radisson from one of the French settlements. Radisson spent several years traveling through upper New York and the Great Lakes region with the Mohawk before returning to the French colony. Soon he set off on a series of adventures beyond the settled frontier: in western New York, Michigan, Minnesota, and eventually Canada. In the 1660s, Radisson went to work for the British. He helped them establish the Hudson's Bay fur-trading company.

Radisson spent his final years in England, where he wrote about his adventures. Here, he describes bison, which were called buffs. These animals were foreign to Europeans. He also sums up his feelings about the North American landscape, which are very different from William Bradford's.

> The buff is a furious animal … The horns of buffs are as those of an ox, but not so long, but bigger and of a blackish color … He is reddish, his hair frizzled and very fine, all parts of his body much unto an

ox. The biggest are bigger than any ox whatsoever ... It's a pleasure to find the place of their abode, for they turn round about, compassing two or three acres of land, beating the snow with the feet and, coming to the center, they lie down and rise again to eat the boughs of trees that they can reach. They go not out of the circle that they have made until hunger compels them ...

The further we sojourned the delightfuller the land was to us. I can say that in my lifetime I never saw a more incomparable country ... The country was so pleasant, so beautiful and fruitful that it grieved me to see the world could not discover such enticing countries to live in. This I say because the Europeans fight for a rock in the sea against each other, or for a sterile and horrid country. Contrariwise, these kingdoms are so delicious and under so temperate a climate, plentiful of all things, the earth bringing forth its fruit twice a year, the people live long and lusty and wise in their way.

—Quoted in Arthur T. Adams, *The Explorations of Pierre Esprit Radisson* (Minneapolis, MN: Ross and Haines, 1961).

CONSIDER THIS

1. Why do you think Radisson considered it a "pleasure" to find the bisons' resting places?
2. To what might Radisson have been referring when he speaks of Europeans fighting over rocks in the sea and "sterile and horrid" countries?

KEY TERMS AND CONCEPTS

From Pierre Esprit Radisson's account:
contrariwise In contrast.
sojourned Stayed somewhere.

From William Call's diary:
canew Canoe.
cats Catfish.
chois Choice.
plaise Place.
prefer Postpone.

A Pioneer's Journal

Great Britain tried to keep the colonists from crossing the Appalachian Mountains to settle in the Ohio River valley after signing the Treaty of Paris, which ended the French and Indian War. That land was designated for the Native Americans. Some colonists, however, kept pushing westward. Many crossed the mountains illegally to settle in the forbidden territory. Among them was Daniel Boone. In March 1775, he led a group of pioneers, or people who are the first to explore a new area or place, into "Caintuck," which we now know as Kentucky. These pioneers built a fort on the Kentucky River and founded a settlement.

William Call was one of the pioneers. He kept a diary of his family's arrival there. In it, he describes how the pioneers used a lottery system to determine which piece of land each family received. The last entry in the diary was written after the Calls ran out of flour. They would have no bread until the crops they planted produced grain the following year. Like the settlers in Jamestown, the Kentucky pioneers soon used up what they had brought with them from home and had to live off the land.

> *THURSDAY 20TH*—this morning is clear and cool. We start early and git Down to caintuck to Boons foart about 12 o'clock where we stop they come out to meet us and welcome us in with a voley of guns.
>
> *FRYDAY 21ST*—warm this Day they begin laying out lots in the town and preparing for people to go to work to make corn.

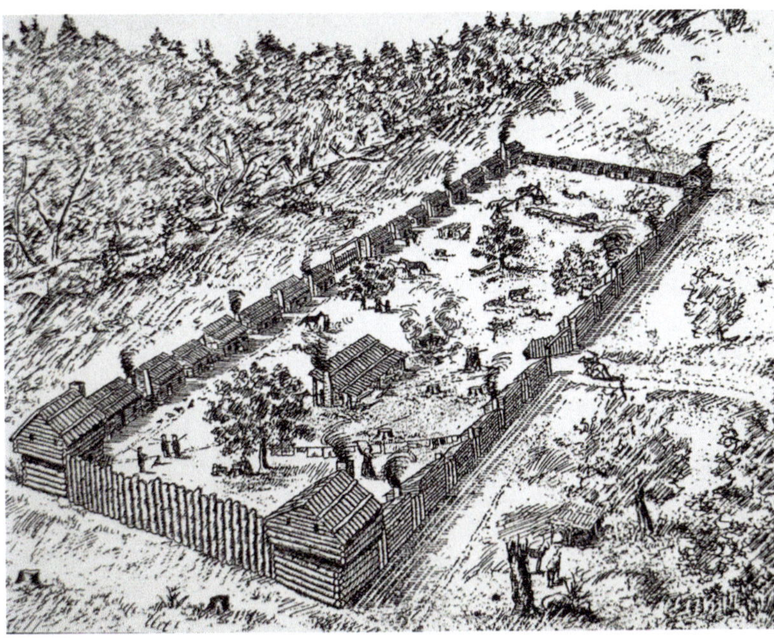

This is a drawing of Fort Boonesborough, built by Daniel Boone and the pioneers he led, as it would have looked in 1778. It was situated near the Kentucky River.

SATTERDAY 22ND—they finish laying out lots this eavening I went a-fishing and caught 3 cats they meet in the night to draw for chois of lots but prefer it till morning.

SUNDAY 23RD—this morning the peopel meets and draws for chois of lots this is a very warm day.

MONDAY 24TH—We all view our lots and some Don't like them about 12 o'clock the combses come to town and Next morning they make them a bark canew and set off down the river to meet their Companey.

TUESDAY 25TH—in the eavening we git us a plaise at the mouth of the creek and begin clearing.

WEDNESDAY 26TH—We Begin Building us a house and a plaise of Defense to Keep the indians off this day we begin to live without bread.

—Quoted in Thomas Speed, *The Wilderness Road: A Description of the Routes of Travel by which the Pioneers and Early Settlers First Came to Kentucky* (Louisville: John P. Morton & Company, 1886).

CONSIDER THIS

1. Does the procedure for giving land to families sound fair to you?
2. What are some of the things you think people ate when the flour ran out?

Only a New World to Some

Slowly but surely, the Europeans in the New World became accustomed to the new landscape and the challenges of establishing new societies. For instance, the people of Plymouth would go on to be a part of the Massachusetts colony—one of the central colonies during the colonial period. It would, however, take time.

As strange and as interesting as this new landscape was for the explorers, pilgrims, and pioneers, it was familiar territory to people who had lived on the land for centuries: the Native Americans.

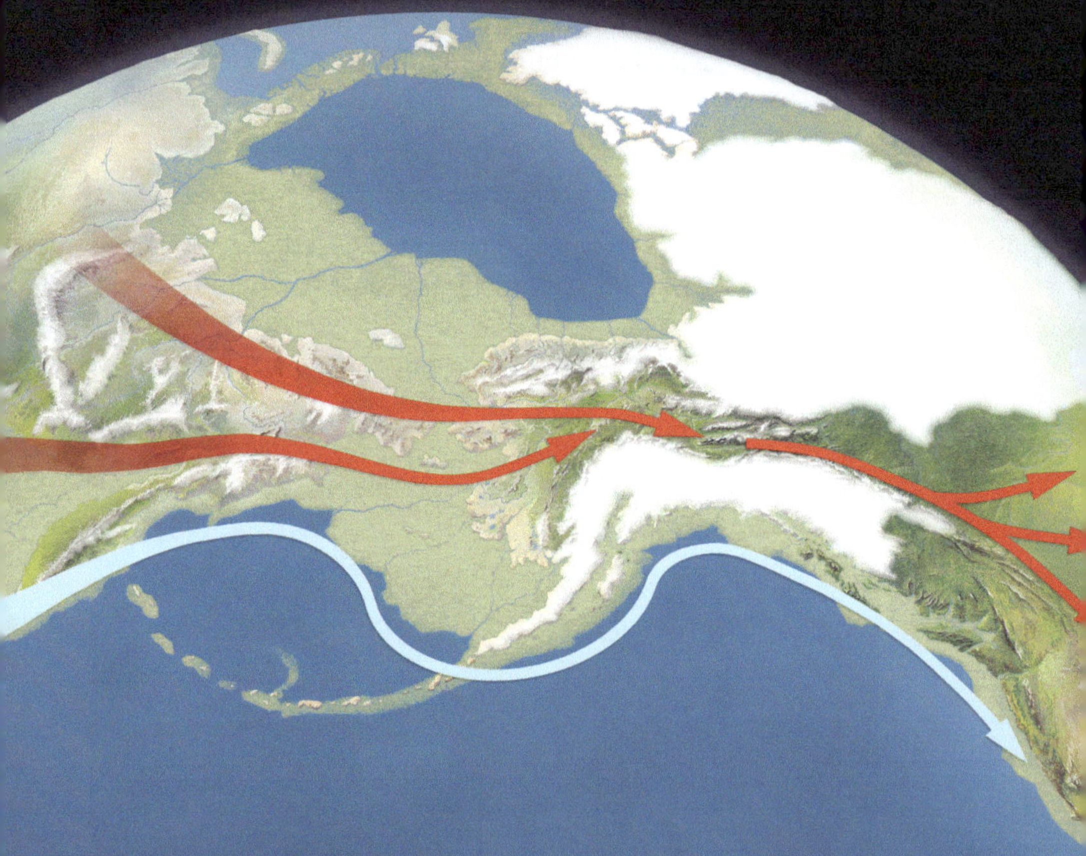

The red arrows on this map depict how Native Americans' ancestors migrated from Asia (*left*) across the Bering Land Bridge, or Beringia (*center*), to North America (*right*) over ten thousand years ago.

3 Natives

Before European explores "discovered" the Americas, there were indigenous, or native, people who lived there. Although historians cannot be sure, they predict that there were millions of Native Americans that lived in the Americas when Europeans arrived in the late fifteenth century. Even the Natives, however, came from elsewhere.

Migration to the Americas

Native Americans' ancestors traveled to America from northeastern Asia a long time ago, although scientists are still not sure exactly when. They estimate, however, that the Native Americans arrived more than ten thousand years ago. They believe Natives arrived during an ice age, when ice covered much of the northern world. The Native Americans were able to travel from northeast Asia using what scientists call the Bering Land Bridge, or Beringia.

This used to be where the Bering Strait is today. The strait, a narrow waterway, separates present-day Russia and the US state of Alaska. Scientists believe these two landmasses used to be connected by the land bridge. Animals and people migrated across it to populate the Americas.

Over the centuries, the people of North America formed hundreds of distinct societies, each with its own language. Their ways of life varied. Some lived in the Arctic and hunted walrus. Some built log houses in the woods, hunted deer, and grew edible plants. Others lived in many-roomed brick structures in the hot, dry Southwest. They survived by using irrigation, or the supply of water through channels, to grow fields of corn, beans, and squash. Despite the diversity of their cultures, all of the Natives had one thing in common. Their worlds would change dramatically when the Europeans arrived.

First Encounters

First meetings between Native Americans and white Europeans took many forms and often involved misunderstandings on both sides. Columbus, for example, called the Natives of the Caribbean "Indians." He mistakenly thought that they were natives of India since he thought he was traveling toward Asia. Although he was wrong, the name stuck. Similarly, the Aztec leader Montezuma II thought that the Spanish conquistador Hernán Cortés was an embodiment, or physical manifestation, of one of the Aztec gods. In reality, Cortés was an invader. He came to destroy Montezuma and his empire.

First meetings, however, could also be far less dramatic. Some were encounters between navigators or fishermen who had come ashore. The Native people were curious about the pale-skinned strangers, their ships, and their strange possessions of steel and glass. Many meetings ended in trade and the beginnings of communication. Friendships, or at least relationships based on mutual respect, did develop.

The Impact

Despite some respectful relationships, the arrival of Europeans was disastrous overall for the Native Americans. Europeans murdered and kidnapped Natives. Other Native Americans died from diseases that Europeans brought with them. For instance, Europeans were used to smallpox and measles. These foreign diseases, however, wiped out whole Native American populations. In addition to murder and disease decimating the Natives, Europeans' desires for westward expansion further threatened the Native Americans' ways of life. By the late seventeenth century, Native Americans actively resisted westward expansion and European aggression.

Face-to-Face

The Pilgrims worried about the dangerous "savages" who "infested" North America. During their first few months at Plymouth, they only caught glimpses of Native Americans in the distance. In March 1621, however, a Native American man introduced himself. He has gone down in history as Samoset, originally from Maine. Samoset introduced the Pilgrims to a local chieftain, or leader of a people, named Massasoit. He was responsible for maintaining peace between the Native Americans and the colonists for many years. The Pilgrims even nursed Massasoit back to health when he was sick in 1623.

Similarly, Samoset introduced the colonists to another Native American named Squanto. He not only spoke English but had been to England. An Englishman named Thomas Hunt had kidnapped Native Americans, including Squanto, from Massachusetts a few years earlier and sold them as slaves in Spain. Squanto somehow escaped, found his way to England, and returned to Massachusetts on a Newfoundland Company ship in 1619. After he returned to find his people had died from European diseases, Squanto served as an interpreter between

Massasoit and the colonists. He helped them build the peace that lasted during Massasoit's lifetime.

This passage from Bradford's history of Plymouth describes the colonists' first meetings with the helpful Natives.

> All this while the Indians came skulking about them, and would sometimes show them selves aloofe off, but when any approached near them, they would rune away. And once they stoale away their tools wher they had been at worke, and were gone to diner. But about the 16. of March a certaine Indian came bouldly amongst them, and spoke to them in broken English, which they could well understand, but marvelled at it. At length they understood by discourse with him, that he was not of these parts, but belonged to the eastrene parts, wher some English-ships came to fish, with whom he was acquainted, and could name sundrie of them by their names, amongst whom he had gott his language. He became profitable to them in acquainting them with many things concerning the state of the cuntry in the east-parts wher he lived, which was afterwards profitable unto them; as also of the people hear, of their names, number, and strength; of their situation and distance from this place, and who was cheefe amongst them. His name was Samaset; he tould them also of another Indian whos name was Squanto, a native of this place, who had been in England and could speake better English than him selfe. Being, after some time of entertainmente and gifts, dismist, a while after he came againe, and 5. more with him, and they brought again all the tooles that were stolen away before, and made way for the coming of their great Sachem, called Massasoyt; who, about 4. or 5. days

> after, came with the cheefe of his friends and other attendance, with the aforesaid Squanto ... Squanto continued with them, and was their interpreter, and was a spetiall instrument sent of God for their good beyond their expectation. He directed them how to set their corne, wher to take fish, and to procure other comodities, and was also their pilott to bring them to unknowne places for their profitt, and never left them till he dyed.
>
> —Reprinted in William T. Davis, ed., *Bradford's History of Plymouth Plantation: 1606-1646* (New York: Charles Scribner's Sons, 1908).

CONSIDER THIS

1. Bradford offered two explanations for the appearance of English-speaking Native Americans at Plymouth. What are they?
2. In what ways did Samoset help the settlers?

Mary Rowlandson Recalls Her Capture

King Philip's War (1675–1676) was a conflict between settlers and Native Americans in New England. King Philip was the English name for Chief Metacom, the son of Massasoit. The conflict technically began over the murder of three of Metacom's men. However, the war was a result of growing tensions between white colonists and the Native Americans.

In November 1675, a thousand colonists attacked a camp of the Narragansett and Nipmuck people in Rhode Island and set it afire. Puritan preacher Increase Mather wrote that "men, women, and Children (no man knoweth how many hundreds of them) were burnt to death." His son Cotton Mather, also a

This image depicts Mary Rowlandson cradling one of her children when the Nipmucks and Narragansetts attacked the Lancaster settlement.

preacher, excitedly reported that the Native Americans had been barbecued.

Three months later, a force of Nipmucks and Narragansetts attacked the settlement of Lancaster, Massachusetts. They were led by Metacom. They took twenty-four captives, including Mary Rowlandson and three of her children. She was separated from her ten-year-old daughter and fourteen-year-old son. Her younger daughter, wounded in the attack, soon died. Rowlandson spent nearly twelve weeks as a servant of her captors before they exchanged her for some trade goods. Soon the Native Americans also released her surviving children. Her account of her experience, *A True History of the Captivity and Restoration of Mrs. Mary Rowlandson*, was published in 1682. It contains the following description of the raid in which she was captured.

> Now is that dreadful Hour come that I have often heard of ... Some in our House were fighting for their Lives, others wallowing in their Blood; the House on fire over our Heads, and the bloody Heathen ready to knock us on the Head if we stirred out. Now might we hear Mothers and Children crying out for themselves and one another, Lord, what shall we do? ... But to return: the Indians laid hold of us, pulling me one way and the Children another, and said, Come go along with us. I told them they would kill me. They

KEY TERMS AND CONCEPTS

From William Bradford's manuscript:

aloofe Aloof, or distant.

commodity A raw material or product.

dismist Dismissed, sent away.

eastrene Eastern.

procure To obtain with care.

sundrie Sundry, an assortment.

From Mary Rowlandson's account:

barbarous Uncivilized or incredibly cruel.

heathen A person who does not belong to a religion and a term used by colonists to describe the Native Americans.

ravenous Extremely hungry.

answered, If I were willing to go along with them they would not hurt me ... I had often before said, that if the Indians should come, I should chuse rather to be killed by them than taken alive; but when I came to the trial my mind changed; their glittering Weapons so daunted my Spirit, that I chose rather to go with those (as I may say) ravenous Bears, than that moment to end my daies ... Now away we must go with those Barbarous Creatures, with our bodies wounded and bleeding, and our hearts no less than our bodies.

—Reprinted in William Andrews, ed., *Journeys in New Worlds: Early American Women's Narratives* (Madison, WI: University of Wisconsin Press, 1990).

CONSIDER THIS

1. Why did Mary Rowlandson agree to go with her captors?

Frustration from the Frontier

In 1764, a year after the French and Indian War ended, the governor of Pennsylvania received a letter from Matthew Smith and James Gibson. They were two farmers on the colony's western frontier. The letter accused the governor of not giving citizens on the edge of the colony the same protections and privileges as those living closer to the capital of Philadelphia. Smith and Gibson wanted to send more representatives to the House of Assembly, the colony's legislature, from the frontier. The legislature was the part of the colonial government responsible for making laws. Smith and Gibson were also interested in issues of justice and punishment for Native Americans on the frontier. They thought the Native Americans responsible for hurting the western communities should not be protected by the colony's laws.

> During the late and present Indian wars, the frontiers of this Province have been repeatedly attacked and ravaged by skulking parties of the Indians, who have with the most savage cruelty murdered men, women, and children without distinction, and have reduced near a thousand families to the most extream distress. It grieves us to the very heart to see such of our frontier inhabitants as have escaped savage fury with the loss of their parents, their children, their

> wives or relatives, left destitute by the public, and exposed to the most cruel poverty and wretchedness while upwards of an hundred and twenty of the savages who are with great reason suspected of being guilty of these horrid barbarities under the mask of friendship, have procured themselves to be taken under the protection of government, with a view to elude the fury of the brave relatives of the murdered, and are now maintained at the public expense.
>
> —Reprinted in Samuel Eliot Morison, *Sources and Documents Illustrating the American Revolution, 1764–1788: And the Formation of the Federal Constitution* (Oxford, UK: Clarendon Press, 1923).

CONSIDER THIS

1. What is the central complaint in the letter?
2. How do you think the men who wrote the letter would have liked to deal with the Native Americans whom the government protected?

Dragging-Canoe's Perspective

Many Native Americans did not use written language in the colonial period. Most of what we know about them comes from the writings of European explorers and colonists. The words that Native Americans are supposed to have spoken often sound very European when translated into English. A Cherokee leader named Dragging-Canoe is said to have made the following speech to his people in 1775. In the speech, he says that they should not have sold their hunting lands to the white people. Even if the wording of the speech is not accurate, it reveals the pride and anger of Native Americans who saw their world being taken away by land-hungry colonists.

> Whole nations have melted away like balls of snow before the sun. The whites have passed the mountains and settled upon Cherokee lands, and now wish to have their usurpation sanctioned by the confirmation of a treaty. New cessions will be required, and the small remnant of my people will be compelled to seek a new retreat in some far distant wilderness. There they will be permitted to stay only a short while, until they again behold the advancing banners of the same greedy hosts. When the whites are unable to point out any farther retreat for the miserable Cherokees, they will proclaim the extinction of the whole race. Should we not therefore run all risks, and incur all consequences, rather than submit to further laceration of our territory? Such treaties may be all right for men too old to hunt or fight. As for me, I have my young warriors about me. We will have our lands.
>
> —Quoted in Robert L. Kinkaid, *The Wilderness Road* (New York: Bobbs-Merrill, 1947).

CONSIDER THIS

1. What future did Dragging-Canoe foresee for his people? Do you think his vision of the future was correct?
2. What was the purpose of Dragging-Canoe's speech? What course of action did he wish to take?

KEY TERMS AND CONCEPTS

From Matthew Smith and James Gibson's letter:

destitute Lacking basic needs.

distress A state of suffering or sorrow.

elude To escape or avoid.

province A colony.

skulking Moving around in a sneaky way.

wretchedness An unhappy or unfortunate state.

From Dragging-Canoe's account:

cession A formal abandonment of property or rights.

compel To require or force.

incur To bring upon oneself.

laceration A cut or wound.

proclaim To announce publicly .

sanctioned Officially allowed or approved.

usurpation A wrongful or illegal occupation.

An Enslavement Attempt

In addition to westward expansion and general aggression, Europeans briefly tried to enslave Native Americans. The colonial economy, especially in the South, relied on manual labor. There simply weren't enough colonists up to the task. They tried to capture and force Native Americans into slave labor. However, high death rates among captured Natives made this a poor solution. Instead, colonists had to seek alternative solutions.

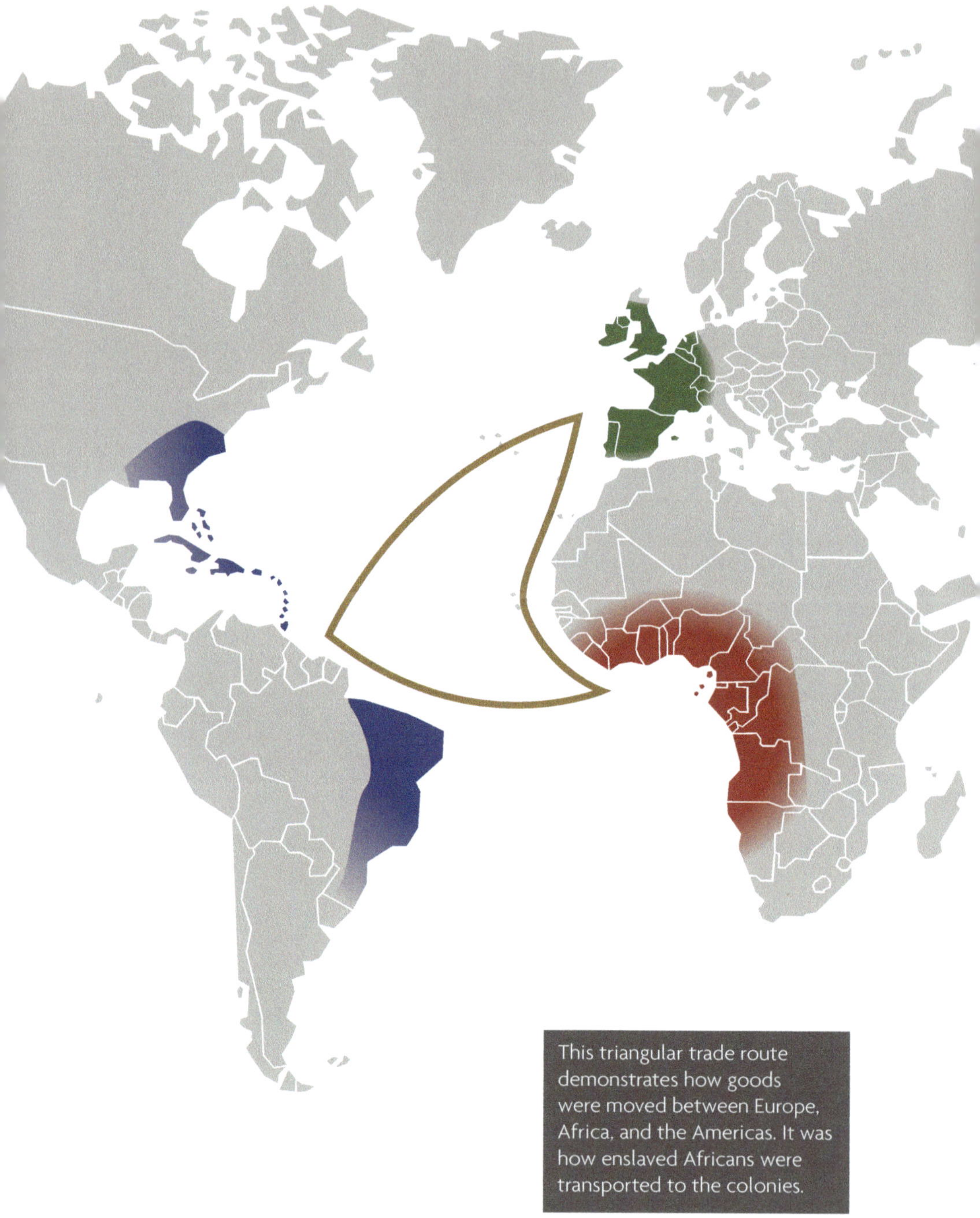

This triangular trade route demonstrates how goods were moved between Europe, Africa, and the Americas. It was how enslaved Africans were transported to the colonies.

4 Enslaved Africans

Agricultural exports became a main part of colonial American economies. Initially, the colonies relied on indentured servants to do the agricultural work. Indentured servants were men and women required, by contract, to work for a person for a fixed amount of time. These servants were other western Europeans. In this system, people who could not afford the high costs of moving to the New World agreed to work for a set period of time for whoever paid their way. These contracts were usually for two to seven years. Masters could sell or trade the labor contracts of these indentured servants, who had few rights under the law. Changing tides in Europe and rules related to slavery, however, led colonists to move away from using indentured servants as a primary labor source. Eventually, colonists determined that slavery was the only way to meet their needs for labor.

The Slave Trade

In the early sixteenth century, Spain began to purchase Africans from African slave merchants on the coast of West Africa. After purchasing these enslaved Africans, the Spanish would take them across the Atlantic to work on Caribbean sugarcane plantations. Other European nations with colonies in the Caribbean and South America, like Portugal, the Netherlands, England, and France, started to do the same. Soon, African slavery was established in the islands and in the South American colonies.

Slave traders would sell enslaved people to the highest bidders. Families were often separated, even mothers from small children.

Slavery in Colonial North America

It was not long before the North American colonists invested in the slave trade as well. In 1619, a ship carrying the region's first enslaved Africans arrived in Virginia. It left about twenty Africans, who were described as "servants." At the time, the term meant either a hired servant or a slave. By 1660, the Virginia colony's population included several hundred Africans.

Although some free Africans owned property and supported themselves by operating businesses or practicing skilled trades such as blacksmithing and carpentry, most Africans were enslaved. In 1670, there were approximately 2,000 enslaved Africans in Virginia and over 20,000 by 1715. By the beginning of the American Revolution in 1775, there were approximately 150,000 enslaved

Africans living in Virginia alone. Slavery was not limited to Virginia, however. The growth of the colonies along the Chesapeake Bay was accompanied by a steady growth in the slave trade.

Slavery existed in all of the colonies, even the Northern ones. However, not everyone approved of the institution. For instance, the Quakers were particularly opposed to it. As time went on, some colonists began to see that slavery was a violent and cruel institution. One of these individuals was Thomas Jefferson, who would become the third president of the United States. He was a plantation owner and slaveholder who became a leader in the British colonies' fight for independence. Jefferson was bothered by slavery but did not know what the alternative to it was. Although he owned over six hundred enslaved Africans during his lifetime, of which he only freed seven, in 1807 he signed a bill making it illegal to bring any more people from Africa to the United States for slave labor.

Despite some people's reservations about the institution, slavery lasted decades after colonists fought for their independence from Britain. Once colonial America became the United States, the enslavement of Africans would continue until the mid-nineteenth century. The Thirteenth Amendment officially abolished, or ended, slavery in 1865.

An Enslaved Man Writes to the Bishop of London

Many enslaved Africans in North America adopted the Christian religion. Some found comfort in it. Some found support for the fact that their enslavement was wrong. In 1723, an enslaved man in Virginia sent the Church of England's new bishop the following letter. He did not sign his name because he feared his owner.

The writer compares those enslaved in America to the Jewish people, referred to as the Children of Israel, in the Bible. They were enslaved in Egypt in ancient times. He begs the bishop to do what he can to improve the condition of those enslaved in the colonies. Unfortunately, this document was misfiled, or incorrectly placed, and the bishop never saw it.

> Our task mastrs ... look no more upon us then if we ware dogs which I hope when these Strange Lines comes to your Lord Ships hands will be looket into ...
>
> We desire that our Childarn be putt to Scool and Larnd to Reed through the Bybell which is all at prasant with our prayers to god for itts good Success before your honour ...
>
> —Quoted in Robin Blackburn, *The Making of New World Slavery: From the Baroque to the Modern, 1492-1800* (London and New York: Verso, 1997).

CONSIDER THIS

1. What improvements does the writer hope for?
2. How do you think he managed to send a letter to the Bishop of London?
3. What do you think might have happened to him if his master discovered this letter?

Slaveholders Fear Rebellion

The slaveholders of British America were aware of the frustrations of enslaved Africans. Many white colonists feared an uprising, or rebellion. This was a major fear in the Southern colonies, where there was the greatest number of slaves. The enslaved laborers there were also often treated worse than in the North.

The two passages below, from letters written in the 1730s, show the concerns of two Virginians. The first was written by a colonial official. In the letter, he discusses how he kept a rebellion from happening by punishing the "Ring-leaders," or the people who would have been in charge of the uprising.

> Here there was a general rumour among [the slaves] that they were to be set free. And when they saw nothing came of it they grew angry and saucy … and talked of rising … But by patroulling; and whipping …, they quietly broke …

The second passage was written by a plantation owner and slaveholder, William Byrd.

> We have … at least ten thousand … of these descendants of Ham fit to bear arms … Should [there] arise a man … exasperated by [slavery], he might with more advantage than Cataline kindle a servile war.
>
> — Quoted in Robin Blackburn, *The Making of New World Slavery: From the Baroque to the Modern, 1492-1800* (London and New York: Verso, 1997).

CONSIDER THIS

1. Do you think that the colonial official's treatment of the "Ring-leaders," as described in the first letter, was justified?
2. What do you think William Byrd's greatest fear was? Do you think he was more afraid of losing his property or his life?

Olaudah Equiano Shares His Story

Olaudah Equiano was born in West Africa around 1745. At age eleven, he was kidnapped by African slave traders. Eventually, he was sold into slavery and loaded onto a slave ship. Equiano's first master gave him the name Gustavus Vassa. For ten years, he was enslaved in England and colonial Pennsylvania.

After obtaining his freedom from a Quaker master, he moved to England to work in the abolition movement. This movement's goal was to end slavery. In 1789, he published *Olaudah Equiano, or Gustavus Vassa, the African, Written by Himself.* These passages describe his capture and experiences on the ship.

> One day, when all our people were gone out to their works as usual, and only I and my dear sister were left to mind the house, two men and a woman got over our walls, and in a moment seized us both, and without giving us time to cry out, or make resistance, they stopped our mouths, and ran off with us into the nearest wood. Here they tied our hands, and continued to carry us as far as they could, till night came on, when we reached a small house, where the robbers halted for refreshment, and spent the night. We were then unbound, but were unable to take any food; and, being quite overpowered by fatigue and grief, our only relief was sleep, which allayed our misfortune for a short time … But alas! we were soon deprived of even the small comfort of weeping together. The next day proved a day of greater sorrow than I had yet experienced; for my sister and I were then separated, while we lay clasped in each other's arms …

KEY TERMS AND CONCEPTS

From the two slaveholders' accounts:

Cataline Lucius Sergius Catilinus, a Roman aristocrat who in 63 BCE tried, unsuccessfully, to overthrow the Roman government with an army that included criminals and peasants (but not slaves).

descendants of Ham In the Bible, Noah curses his son Ham's descendants to forever be servants of one of his brothers; Ham was thought to be the forefather of Africans. This curse was used by colonists as a reason to justify the enslavement of Africans.

exasperated Intensely irritated.

kindle To start.

saucy Disrespectful.

servile war A slave rebellion.

One day [the crew] had taken a number of fishes; and when they had killed and satisfied themselves with as many as they thought fit, to our astonishment who were on deck, rather than give any of them to us to eat, as we expected, they tossed the remaining fish into the sea again, although we begged and prayed for some as well as we could, but in vain; and some of my countrymen, being pressed by hunger, took an opportunity, when they thought no one saw them, of trying to get a little privately; but they were discovered, and the attempt procured them some very

> severe floggings. One day, when we had a smooth sea and moderate wind, two of my wearied countrymen who were chained together (I was near them at the time), preferring death to such a life of misery, somehow made through the nettings and jumped into the sea; immediately, another quite dejected fellow, who, on account of his illness, was suffered to be out of irons, also followed their example; and I believe many more would very soon have done the same, if they had not been prevented by the ship's crew, who were instantly alarmed ... [T]wo of the wretches were drowned, but they got the other, and afterwards flogged him unmercifully, for thus attempting to prefer death to slavery.
>
> —Reprinted in Arna Bontemps, ed., *Great Slave Narratives* (Boston: Beacon Press, 1969).

CONSIDER THIS

1. Do you think this account was useful to the abolitionist movement?
2. How do you feel about the enslaved individuals who jumped into the ocean? Do you understand why, as Equiano said, they preferred "death to such a life of misery"?

Nobody but God: Elizabeth's Story

For many Africans in North America, one of the cruelest parts of slavery was being forced apart from their loved ones. Some faced the same fate as Elizabeth. She was born to enslaved parents in Maryland in 1766. Since children of enslaved women were automatically enslaved, Elizabeth immediately became a slave.

However, she obtained her freedom when she was thirty. She lived to be a very old woman. In the 1860s, during the Civil War, she published the story of her early years.

> In the eleventh year of my age, my master sent me to another farm, several miles from my parents, brothers, and sisters, which was a great trouble to me. At last I grew so lonely and sad I thought I should die, if I did not see my mother. I asked the overseer if I might go, but being positively denied, I concluded to go without his knowledge. When I reached home my mother was away. I set off and walked twenty miles before I found her. I staid with her for several days, and we returned together. Next day I was sent back to my new place, which renewed my sorrow. At parting, my mother told me that I had "nobody in the wide world to look to but God." I went back repeating as I went, "none but God in the wide world." On reaching the farm, I found the overseer was displeased at me for going without his liberty. He tied me with a rope, and gave me some stripes [lashes] of which I carried the marks for weeks.
>
> —Reprinted in Henry Louis Gates, ed., *Six Women's Slave Narratives* (New York: Oxford University Press, 1988).

CONSIDER THIS

1. What are some reasons why slaveholders might have separated enslaved individuals from their families?
2. What role do you think religion played in the lives of Elizabeth and her mother?

Equiano was kidnapped and sold into slavery like many Africans. However, he eventually was able to purchase his freedom.

KEY TERMS AND CONCEPTS

From Olaudah Equiano's autobiography:

allayed Lessened.

dejected Sad or depressed.

flog To beat someone.

wearied Tired.

From Elizabeth's memoir:

liberty Permission.

overseer A person on a plantation that supervises the slaves.

Just One Element

Despite horrific and heartbreaking accounts like Elizabeth's and Equiano's, slavery continued throughout colonial America. Although many colonists were reliant on slave labor, slavery was just one part of everyday life in the colonies.

Life in the colonies wasn't easy. Here, a settler distributes a small amount of corn. This drawing depicts a time when the Jamestown settlement feared possible starvation.

5 *Everyday Life in the Colonies*

British North America was overwhelmingly rural and agricultural throughout the colonial period. Although many of us may think about the founding of large settlements and key people like William Penn or John Smith, there were many ordinary people who moved to the countryside. The majority of them were farmers or laborers on farms owned by other people.

Rural and Urban Living

The typical colonial family lived in an isolated farmhouse. Families worked together on farms, in stores, and in workshops. They made goods such as clothes and candles for themselves. They visited the marketplaces of the nearest village or town once a month or so. They went to church weekly or more often if they could. If they couldn't make it to services, they held family prayers and Bible readings.

But the modern image of the colonial village, complete with white steeples and tidy houses clustered around a central green, is not a myth. Such centers did form, especially in New England. There and in other parts of the colonies, some communities grew into towns and even cities. Almost from its beginning, New Amsterdam—later New York City—was a busy urban center. A lot of the activity was because of its port. Other ports also grew into major colonial cities. For instance, by the end of the colonial period, Philadelphia had at least thirty thousand inhabitants. It was one of the most important cities in the British Empire.

Other Differences

Although the colonies were primarily agricultural, farming styles varied from place to place. The southern colonies practiced plantation agriculture, growing large amounts of crops such as tobacco, rice, and cotton. They sold these crops to merchants who exported them. The middle colonies also grew cash crops for sale, but they mainly produced wheat. They also marketed livestock. In New England, the growing seasons were shorter and the soil was not as fertile, or good for crops. People farmed minimally and only produced food crops for their own use.

Throughout the colonies, daily life for most people centered on work. If people weren't working the land, they were working by sharing their crafts and taking care of their families. That said, life did look very different for the few that were rich enough to be idle.

Folk Medicine and Remedies

Doctors were rare in colonial America, especially in the early years. When sickness struck, most people treated themselves and their families. They depended upon folk medicine, traditional remedies, and cures passed down from generation to generation.

Colonists would have relied on their immediate and extended families to help with daily tasks around the farm and house, such as feeding livestock and cleaning.

The following folk remedies from the seventeenth century show how people treated common medical problems. The first one is about using the root of the sassafras tree as a health tonic. The second describes how to treat the swelling caused by a toothache. The third offers a treatment for styes, or swellings on the eyelids.

Health Tonic Remedy:

In the spring of the year,
When the blood is too thick,
There is nothing so rare
As the sassafras stick.
It cleans up the liver,

> It strengthens the heart,
> And to the whole system
> New life doth impart.
> Sassafras, oh, sassafras!
> Thou art the stuff for me!
> And in the spring I love to sing
> Sweet sassafras! of thee.
>
> —Quoted in David Freeman Hawke, *Everyday Life in Colonial America* (New York: Harper and Row, 1988).

Remedy for Toothache Swelling:

> They boil gruel of maize and milk; to this they add, whilst it is yet over the fire, some of the fat of hogs or other suet and stir it well, that everything mix equally. A handkerchief is then spread over the gruel and applied as hot as possible to the swelled cheek, where it is kept till it is gone cool again.
>
> —Quoted in David Freeman Hawke, *Everyday Life in Colonial America* (New York: Harper and Row, 1988).

Remedy for Styes:

> A small and pleasant craft of the blacksmith was to remove styes from the eyes of children. They were sent to him to ask him to do it, and he'd say, "Just wait till I've done this horseshoe," and the child would push close to watch, close to the heat and the steam, and blink hard, every time the great hammer came down with a bang—till in half an hour the smith

would wipe his hands, and look, and smile (for the stye had burst and wept itself away).

—Quoted in David Freeman Hawke, *Everyday Life in Colonial America* (New York: Harper and Row, 1988).

CONSIDER THIS

1. Do you think that most households would have been able to use these methods? Would they have had the necessary ingredients or tools at hand?
2. Why do you think the author of the third account says removing styes is a "pleasant craft"?

One Brave Girl

Some colonial sports and entertainment may seem cruel to us today. Bullbaiting was one such sport. It was a game in which people watched dogs attack a bull. It was a sport from England that was popular in America. Colonial Americans did not have the same beliefs about animal cruelty and animal rights that we have now. In this next passage, a Philadelphia man writes about a surprising occurrence at a bull bait in the middle of the eighteenth century.

The animal was in a great rage, tho' much exhausted before I reached the scene of action. Soon after I got there, the bull threw a small mastiff about ten foot high, which he hooked in the upper jaw and tore it nearly off with every tooth in it. A new pack of dogs were now prepared for the combat, and every eye turned toward them.

At this moment who should break through the ring suddenly but the beautiful Polly Heffernan (for that was her name). She was beholding the battle through the cracks of the high fence which closed the field on South Street, and pitying the persecuted animal she scaled it unseen by the crowd, which she pierced like a dart, and run directly up to the bull, without shoes or stockings on, her bosom bare and her ringlets of beautiful black hair flowing in wild disorder upon her neck and shoulders. Her clothing was nothing but her long shift and a white petticoat, so that ... she appeared more like a ghost than a human being.

When she reached the bull, which almost immediately before was in a great rage, he dropped his ears and bowing his head as if he knew his deliverer was come, she thus accosted him:

"Poor bully! And have they hurt thee? They shall not hurt thee any more," and stroking his forehead she repeated, "They shall not hurt thee any more."

We multitude were confounded and dumbstruck with amazement. Not a man dared to enter the ring to save her, but all stood trembling for Polly's life. In the midst of their gaze, she darted back like an arrow from the bow, over the fence, and returned to the hospital from which she eloped and here the bait ended.

—Quoted in David Freeman Hawke, *Everyday Life in Colonial America* (New York: Harper and Row, 1988).

KEY TERMS AND CONCEPTS

From the folk remedies:

doth impart Is granted.

gruel A thin liquid meal boiled in milk or water.

maize Corn.

suet Hard fat used to make puddings and pastries.

From the bullbaiting account:

accosted Approached someone (or something) boldly.

beholding Watching.

deliverer A person who rescues someone from harm, usually used in a religious sense.

petticoat A smock or a type of undergarment worn under a skirt or dress.

shift A loose-fitting undergarment.

CONSIDER THIS

1. Why do you think the bait ended after Polly Heffernan's surprising appearance?
2. Do you think people in attendance that day attended other bull baits?

Life in the Backcountry: A Missionary's Diary

In 1775 and 1776, just as the American Revolution was beginning, a twenty-eight-year-old New Jersey man named Philip Vickers Fithian traveled through western Virginia, Maryland, and Pennsylvania. He was a missionary, or a traveling preacher, spreading the word of the Presbyterian church. He preached in towns that did not have ministers.

Fithian's journal of the trip is a gentle, often humorous look at everyday life in the frontier settlements. Colonial Americans called these settlements "the backcountry." In this diary entry, Fithian describes a nameless hamlet, or small village, tucked away in a western Pennsylvania valley.

Thursday August 10

Cleanliness & Smartness are visible in our little Hamlet.—All is suitable but this going to Bed & rising in the same Room, & often in full view, of the whole Family—This, to be sure, puts me often to the Blush.

We have here no Meat of any kind. Our Breakfasts are Milk, with Bread & Butter; with these at Dinner we have the Addition of Cymbalines—And for Supper we have only Paste & Milk. It is a rich Repast we have with these original and natural Supports to Life, Health & Vivacity—I feel brisk & vigorous; & am, surely, growing fat, I fear corpulent, upon these natural Luxuries. Simplicity in Living, & Health—Much Carnage in Diet, & several Kinds at the same Time, & all highly, & differently seasoned; Great Quantity & Variety of strong Liquors, which grow poisonous by untimely & immoderate Application—

These stop up & darken the Understanding, they effect that Languor & burdensome Dullness which makes Life & all her Duties appear to many tiresome beyond Measure.

Thompson who came over the Mountains with me is a Droll. Last Night our Fire was almost out.—"Peggy," quoth he, "bring in some Bark to save the Fire"—"Indeed, Tom," answered the Girl, "I am tired, pulling Flax all Day, & cant."—"Well then," quo' Tom, "run out & call in the Neighbours to see it die."

I observe among the People here, & Mr. Fleming tells me it is universal, the greatest Plainness & Familiarity in Conversation; every Man, in all Companies, with almost no Exception, Calls his Wife, Brother, Neighbour, or Acquaintance, by their proper Name of Sally, John, James, or Michael, without ever prefixing the customary Compliment, of "My Dear," Sir, Mr. &c.

—Reprinted in Robert G. Albion, ed., *Philip Vickers Fithian: Journal, 1775–1776* (Princeton, NJ: Princeton University Press, 1934).

CONSIDER THIS

1. How would you describe Fithian's attitude toward life in the country?
2. What did Fithian mean by "Plainness and Familiarity in Conversation"? Do you think he thought this was an admirable quality of the people he met?

"Utmost Hardship": Elizabeth Ashbridge's Story

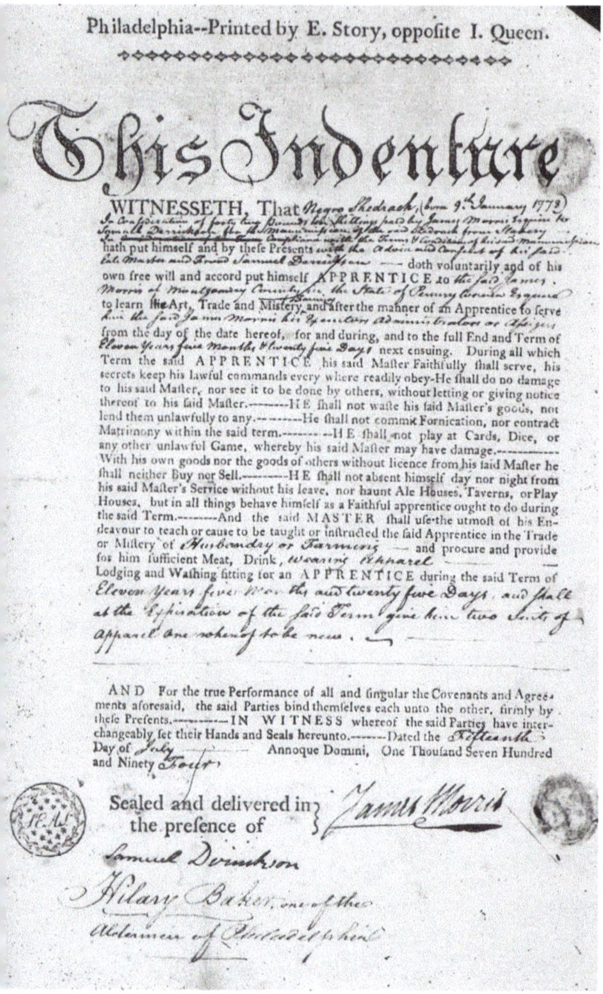
Philadelphia--Printed by E. Story, oppoſite I. Queen.

This Indenture

WITNESSETH, That Negro Shedrach, (born 9th January 1778) [illegible] hath put himſelf and by theſe Preſents [illegible] doth voluntarily and of his own free will and accord put himſelf APPRENTICE to the said James Morris of Montgomery County in the State of Pennsylvania Esquire to learn the Art, Trade and Miſtery, and after the manner of an Apprentice to ſerve him the said James Morris his Executors Administrators or Assigns from the day of the date hereof, for and during, and to the full End and Term of Eleven Years five Months & twenty five Days next enſuing. During all which Term the ſaid APPRENTICE his ſaid Maſter Faithfully ſhall ſerve, his ſecrets keep his lawful commands every where readily obey-He ſhall do no damage to his ſaid Maſter, nor ſee it to be done by others, without letting or giving notice thereof to his ſaid Maſter.--------HE ſhall not waſte his ſaid Maſter's goods, nor lend them unlawfully to any.---------He ſhall not commit Fornication, nor contract Matrimony within the ſaid term.----------HE ſhall not play at Cards, Dice, or any other unlawful Game, whereby his ſaid Maſter may have damage.------------ With his own goods nor the goods of others without licence from his ſaid Maſter he ſhall neither Buy nor Sell.----------HE ſhall not abſent himſelf day nor night from his ſaid Maſter's Service without his leave, nor haunt Ale Houſes, Taverns, or Play Houſes, but in all things behave himſelf as a Faithful apprentice ought to do during the ſaid Term.---------And the ſaid MASTER ſhall uſe the utmoſt of his Endeavour to teach or cauſe to be taught or inſtructed the ſaid Apprentice in the Trade or Miſtery of Husbandry or Farming -- and procure and provide for him ſufficient Meat, Drink, wearing Apparel -- Lodging and Waſhing fitting for an APPRENTICE during the ſaid Term of Eleven Years five Months and twenty five Days, and shall at the Expiration of the said Term give him two Suits of apparel one whereof to be new.

AND For the true Performance of all and ſingular the Covenants and Agreements aforeſaid, the ſaid Parties bind themſelves each unto the other, firmly by theſe Preſents.----------IN WITNESS whereof the ſaid Parties have interchangeably ſet their Hands and Seals hereunto.-------Dated the Fifteenth Day of July Annoque Domini, One Thouſand Seven Hundred and Ninety Four.

Sealed and delivered in the preſence of

James Morris

Samuel Dorickson

Hilary Baker, one of the [illegible]

The term of indentured servitude could vary in length. However, passage to the United States and the promise to feed, clothe, and house the servant were often parts of the contract.

A great number of the people who came to British America did so in some form of bondage. Some were enslaved, especially Africans. Most Europeans, however, came as indentured servants. Anywhere between one-half to two-thirds of the colonial Americans found themselves in this type of bondage. The indentured servant system provided much-needed labor for the growing colonies.

However, the life of an indentured servant could be hard. Elizabeth Ashbridge's story shows that. A ship's captain offered her passage from Ireland to New York in 1732. However, when she arrived, he made her sign an indenture to pay what she owed him. Later in life, Ashbridge became a Quaker missionary. She returned to Ireland and wrote an account of her life. This passage begins with the captain's threats in New York.

> I therefore in a fright Signed [the indenture], & tho' there was no Magistrate present, I being Ignorant in such Cases, it Did well enough to Make me a Servant four Years.
>
> In Two Weeks time I was Sold, & Were it Possible to Convey in Characters a sense of the Sufferings of my Servitude, it would make the most strong heart pity the Misfortunes of a young creature as I was, who had a Tender Education; for tho' my Father had no great Estate, yet he Lived well. I had been used to Little but my School, but now it had been better for me if I had been brought up to more hardship. For a While I was Pretty well used, but in a Little time the Scale turned, Occasioned by a Difference that happened between my Master & me, wherein I was Innocent: from that time he set himself against me and was Inhuman. He would not suffer me to have Clothes to be Decent in, having to go barefoot in his Service in the Snowey Weather & the Meanest Drudgery, wherein I suffered the Utmost Hardship that my Body was able to Bear, which, with the afforesaid Troubles, had like to have been my Ruin to all Eternity had not Almighty God in Mercy Interposed.
>
> —Reprinted in William Andrews, ed., *Journeys in New Worlds: Early American Women's Narratives* (Madison, WI: University of Wisconsin Press, 1990).

KEY TERMS AND CONCEPTS

From Philip Vickers Fithian's journal:

carnage Meat.

corpulent Overweight.

cymbalines Doughnuts.

droll An entertainer or buffoon.

flax A crop harvested for its seeds and its stalks, which can make fabric.

languor The state of tiredness.

paste Porridge or gruel.

repast A meal.

From Elizabeth Ashbridge's account:

afforesaid Previously mentioned.

drudgery Hard work.

in a fright Out of fear.

interpose To intervene.

magistrate A judge or civil officer.

suffer To allow.

tender education A modest education.

CONSIDER THIS

1. Do you think the indenture system was fair? Why or why not?
2. Why do you think her master would not allow her "decent" clothing?

The Nuclear Family

Despite the newness of life in the New World, domestic life during the colonial period was somewhat similar to life across the Atlantic. For instance, the British and the colonists shared the common belief that the nuclear family was the most important unit of society. A nuclear family consists of a married couple and their children. An individual's family determined his or her social status and was a large portion of his or her personal identity. Families' social statuses also determined the types of lives they would lead and the way their children would be raised.

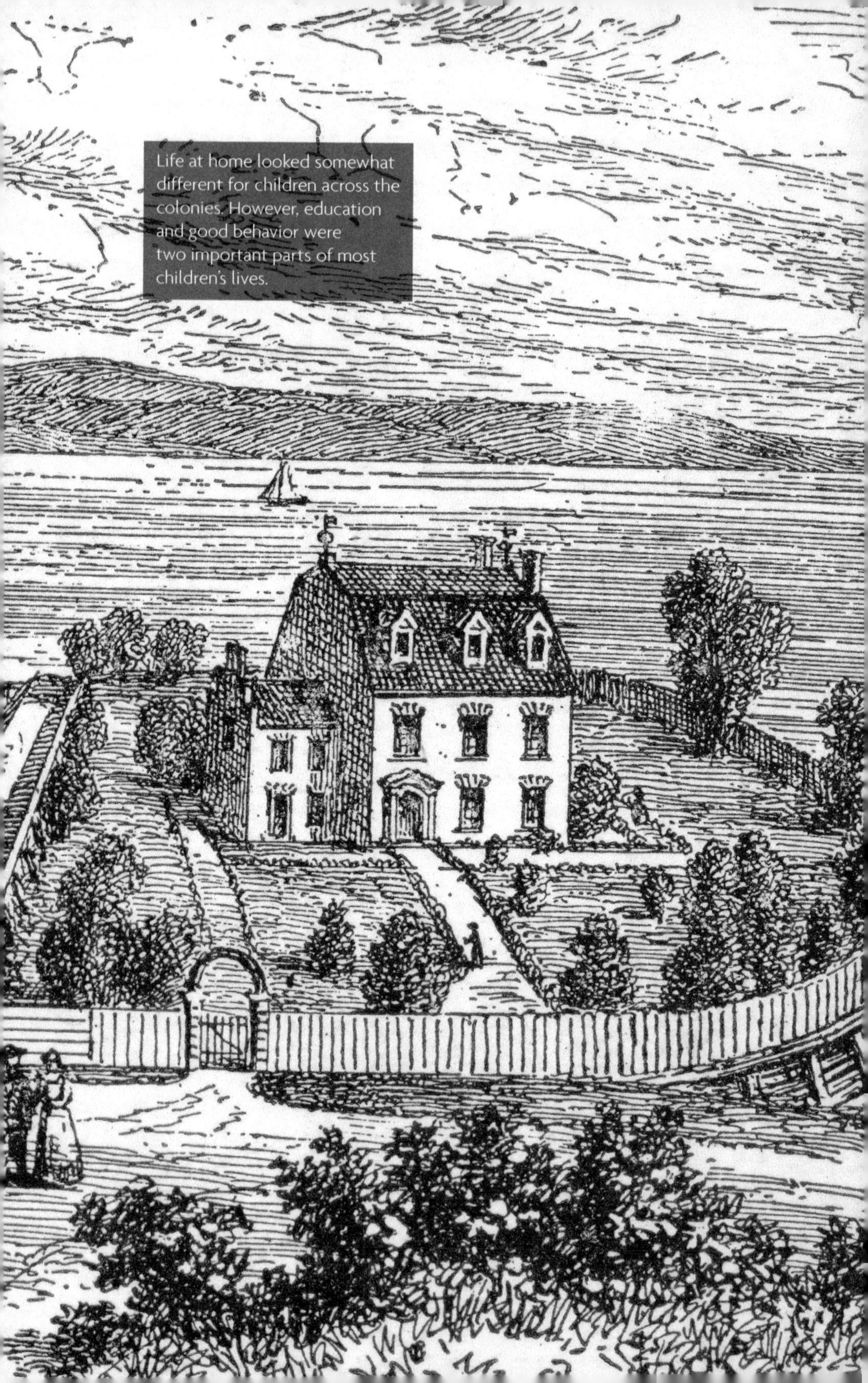

Life at home looked somewhat different for children across the colonies. However, education and good behavior were two important parts of most children's lives.

6 Childhood and Education

Although colonists shared a belief in nuclear families with Britain, often colonial households expanded to include people other than those in the nuclear family. Colonial families tended to be large, and households were generally crowded. It was rare for a child to have his or her own bed, let alone room. Older parents, orphaned family members, and servants often lived with families. Sometimes the line between servants and relatives was blurred. It was common for poor families to send a son or daughter to live with and work for a relative with more money.

Colonial Families and Children

Although many of these aspects of life looked similar to life on the British Isles, British colonists faced dangers they had not known across the ocean. In some areas, Native American wars were a danger. In the Chesapeake Bay area and farther south, diseases such as malaria and typhus cost many colonists their lives. Most families lost several children in infancy. The high death rate overall meant that many young people were orphaned and grew up with relatives, family friends, or foster parents.

Overall, colonial family life relied on the authority of men. Fathers and husbands had a lot of control over their children and wives. Once children reached the age of seven or so, however, they had responsibilities. Girls cared for their younger siblings and helped their mothers with tasks such as gardening and spinning wool. Boys helped their fathers with planting and harvesting, taking care of livestock, or cutting firewood.

By the time young people were teenagers, they were considered valuable sources of labor. Girls might earn money by working for other families as servants. Boys might be apprenticed, or sent to work for a professional or craftsman in exchange for training in a trade.

A boy eventually grew up and developed his own legal identity. However, a girl's father was legally responsible for her until she married. Once she married, her husband became legally responsible for her. Women never had their own legal identities. Married women could not own property, make wills, or sign contracts on their own. Women whose husbands had died, however, had more independence unless they remarried.

The Importance of Education

Before reaching adulthood, education was a part of children's lives in the colonies, although ideas about education would vary from place to place. New England led the way in educational achievement, partly because the Puritans placed a high value on literacy, or the ability to read and write. As early as 1647, Puritans in Massachusetts made a law requiring each community with fifty or more families to have a teacher to teach literacy skills.

This law also made people in the community responsible for the teacher's salary.

Other parts of the colonies were not so quick to establish public education. Some of the wealthiest colonists sent their children to private academies or even to England. But many colonists, especially the rural population, learned to read and write at home, taught by their parents with the Bible as a schoolbook. Others had only a few years or even months of formal education. These individuals saw education as a community responsibility.

Overall, though, whether or not a child received a formal education, he or she was expected to be on his or her best behavior, to act like a little adult.

Proper Behavior: A Rule Book

Colonial Americans were very concerned with courtesy and manners. Rudeness was seen as a threat to the order of the whole community. Records of lawsuits show that people frequently went to court for such violations as name-calling and making faces. For these reasons, parents worked hard to teach their children to act properly.

Ideas about good etiquette and manners were based on the customs of gentlemen and gentlewomen. People turned to handbooks that outlined proper behavior for children. A handbook called *The School of Manners* was published in London in 1701. It became very popular with parents in the American colonies. Among its instructions to the young were the following mealtime rules:

> Never sit down at the table till asked, and after the blessing.
> Ask for nothing; tarry till it be offered thee.
> Speak not.
> Sing not, hum not, wriggle not.
> Bite not thy bread but break it.

Take not salt with a greasy knife.
Dip not the meat in the same [the salt].
Look not earnestly at any other that is eating.
Spit not, cough not, nor blow thy nose at table if it may be avoided; but if there be necessity, do it aside, and without much notice.
Lean not thy elbow on the table, or on the back of thy chair.
Stuff not thy mouth so as to fill thy cheeks; be content with smaller mouthfuls.
Blow not thy meat, but with patience wait till it be cool.
Eat not too fast nor with greedy behavior.
Eat not vastly but moderately.
Make not noise with thy tongue, mouth, lips, or breath in thy eating and drinking.
Smell not of thy meat; nor put it to thy nose; turn it not to the other side upward on thy plate.
When moderately satisfied, leave the table.

—Quoted in Alice Morse Earle, *Child Life in Colonial Days* (New York: Macmillan, 1899).

CONSIDER THIS

1. How do these rules of etiquette compare with the way people eat today?
2. What do the rules tell us about the kinds of food people ate and the way they ate them?

Children could be seen dressed as miniature versions of the adults in their lives. They also learned how to behave like little adults.

A Well-Dressed Boy and Girl

Colonial boys and girls wore long smocks, called petticoats or coats, until they were about six years old. Under these, they wore linen underclothing. Over them, children wore woolen shawls or overshirts for warmth in cold weather. At about age six, children began wearing clothes that were miniature versions of adult garments. Boys wore tight-fitting pants called breeches or britches. Girls wore dresses.

The following lists show the kinds of clothes worn by children of gentlemen. Children from humbler families wore similar clothes. They were made of coarser fabrics such as burlap, homespun linen, or wool. The first list was made in the late 1600s. It shows the clothing ordered for a ten-year-old boy who was being sent away to school. The list mentions osenbrig, stuff, and serge, which are types of cloth. Cravats are ties, and a wastecoat, or waistcoat, is a vest.

The second list dates from 1761. George Washington wrote it when he ordered clothes from London for his six-year-old stepdaughter. Lawn, cambrick, callimanco, and worsted are types of cloth. A frock is a dress. A capuchin is a long cloak with a hood. Egrettes or aigrettes are ornaments worn pinned to the hair or to hats.

> Eleven new shirts, 4 pair laced sleeves, 8 Plane cravats, 4 Cravats with Lace, 4 Stripte Wastecoats with black buttons, 1 Flowered Wastecoat, 4 New osenbrig Britches, 1 Gray hat with a black ribbon, 1 Gray hat with a blew ribbon, 1 Dousin black buttons, 1 Dousin coloured buttons, 3 Pair gold buttons, 3 Pair silver buttons, 2 Pair Fine blew Stockings, 1 Pair Fine red Stockings, 4 White Handkerchiefs, 2 Speckled Handkerchiefs, 5 Pair Gloves, 1 Stuff Coat with black buttons, 1 Cloth Coat, 1 Pair blew plush britches, 1 Pair Serge britches, 2 Combs, 1 Pair new Shooes, Silk & Thred to mend his Cloathes.
>
> —Shirley Glubok, ed., *Home and Child Life in Colonial Days* (New York: Macmillan, 1969).
>
> 1 Coat made of Fashionable Silk. A Fashionable Cap or fillet with Bib apron. Ruffles and Tuckers, to be laced. 4 Fashionable Dresses made of Long Lawn. 2 Fine Cambrick Frocks. A Satin Capuchin, hat, and neckatees. A Persian Quilted Coat. 1 p. Pack Thread Stays. 4 p. Callimanco Shoes. 6 p. Leather Shoes. 2 p. Satin Shoes with flat ties. 6 p. Fine Cotton Stockings. 4 p. White Worsted Stockings. 12 p. Mitts. 6 p. White Kid Gloves. 1 p. Silver Shoe Buckles. 1 p. Neat Sleeve buttons. 6 Handsome Egrettes Different Sorts. 6 Yards Ribbon for Egrettes. 12 Yards Coarse Green Callimanco.

—Quoted in Alice Morse Earle, *Child Life in Colonial Days* (New York: Macmillan, 1899).

CONSIDER THIS

1. What are the differences between these wardrobes and the typical clothes of a boy or girl today?

A Rural Education

Abraham Pierson was born in Killingworth, Connecticut, in 1756. As he was growing up, he kept a journal describing his childhood and education. Young people in the colonies often had to help their parents work on their farms or in their stores or workshops. Like many children, Pierson did not go to school regularly. He managed to learn quite a lot, however, with the help of his parents.

> While I was young I had but little opportunity of going to School having Sometimes not more than 5 or 6 weeks Schooling in a year and at most not more than 10 weeks and many years there was no School at all but notwithstanding the little Schooling I had yet being instructed by my Parents I became able when about 7 years old to read tolerable well in a Bible So as that when I was 8 years old I had almost read the Bible through. I read once every morning Constantly when there was no School and began to learn to write and within a few years I made Some Progress in Arithmetic learn'd the Ground Rules and Several other Useful Rules.

—Quoted in Jacob Ernest Cooke, ed., *Encyclopedia of the North American Colonies,* Volume 2 (New York: Scribner's, 1993).

CONSIDER THIS

1. What kinds of knowledge did Pierson gain as a child?
2. How would you compare his education with the type of education you receive today?

A Boy's Letter to His Father

This 1796 portrait of John Quincy Adams was completed twenty years after he wrote the quoted letter to his father and nearly thirty years before he became president.

In the colonies, educated people wrote many letters. Husbands and wives often wrote each other letters, even when they were not separated. Parents and children did the same. A nine-year-old Massachusetts boy named John Quincy Adams wrote the following letter to his father. His father was lawyer and patriot John Adams. In the late colonial period, a patriot was someone who supported the thirteen colonies' independence from England.

John Adams was a part of the Continental Congress meeting in Philadelphia during the American Revolution. The Congress was not specifically a governing body like a legislature, but it was a political body. Its goal was to express the colonists' concerns to Great Britain and to protect their interests.

Twenty years after receiving this letter, John Adams would become the second president of the United States. Then, in 1825, John Quincy Adams would become the sixth president. The letter was written long before those public events. It shows the respectful affection of the son for the father. It also shows how important education and self-improvement were in the Adams household.

> Braintree, June the 2nd, 1777
>
> Dear Sir:
>
> I love to receive letters very well, much better than I love to write them. I make but a poor figure at composition, my head is much too fickle, my thoughts are running after bird's eggs, play, and trifles until I get vexed with myself. I have but just entered the 3rd vol. of Smollett tho' I had design'd to have got it half through by this time. I have determined this week to be more diligent, as Mr. Thaxter will be absent at Court, & I cannot persue my other studies. I have set myself a Stent & determine to read the Volume Half out. If I can but keep my resolution, I will write again at the end of the week and give a better account of myself. I wish, Sir, you would give me some instructions with regard to my time & advise me how to proportion my Studies & my Play, in writing I will keep them by me & endeavour to follow them. I am, dear Sir, with a present determination of growing better yours. P.S. Sir, if you will be so good as to favour me with a Blank Book, I will transcribe the most remarkable occurrences I meet with in my reading which will serve to fix them upon my mind.

—Reprinted in Alice Morse Earle, *Child Life in Colonial Days* (New York: Macmillan, 1899).

CONSIDER THIS

1. What criticisms does the letter writer make of his own behavior?
2. How does he think his father can help him improve?

Benjamin Franklin's Proposal

During the course of the eighteenth century, Benjamin Franklin dipped into almost every part of intellectual and public life in the colonies. Born in 1706, by the age of forty-two he was wealthy enough to dedicate the rest of his long life to what he called "philosophical studies and amusement." Franklin turned his

Pierre du Simitière, a patriot and artist, made this 1780 sketch of the Academy and College of Philadelphia, which would eventually become the University of Pennsylvania.

attention to scientific experiments, writing, civic projects, and politics. He also owned eighteen mills where paper was made.

Long before Franklin rose to national fame, he took an interest in the affairs of Philadelphia, his home city. In 1749, he published a pamphlet titled *Proposals Relating to the Education of Youth in Pensilvania*. It was a request for help to establish an academy. He was successful. Two years later, the academy opened. Today, it is the University of Pennsylvania.

> The good education of youth has been esteemed by wise men in all ages, as the surest foundation of the happiness both of private families and of commonwealths. Almost all governments have therefore made it a principal object of their attention, to establish and endow with proper revenues, such seminaries of learning, as might supply the succeeding age with men qualified to serve the publick with honour to themselves, and to their country.
>
> Many of the first settlers of these provinces were men who had received a good education in Europe, and to their wisdom and good management we owe much of our present prosperity. But their hands were full, and they could not do all things. The present race are not thought to be generally of equal ability: For though the American youth are allowed not to want capacity; yet the best capacities require cultivation, it being truly with them, as with the best ground, which unless well tilled and sowed with profitable seed, produces only ranker weeds …
>
> —Reprinted in Esmond Wright, ed., *Benjamin Franklin: His Life as He Wrote It* (Cambridge, MA: Harvard University Press, 1996).

KEY TERMS AND CONCEPTS

From John Quincy Adams's letter:

fickle Changeable or inconstant.

proportion Balance.

stent A stint, or amount of work to be completed in a given time.

trifles Unimportant things.

From Benjamin Franklin's *Proposals*:

cultivation A good education.

endow To give.

ranker More unpleasant.

revenue Money.

seminary of learning A college.

sow To plant seeds.

till To prepare soil for planting.

CONSIDER THIS

1. According to Franklin, why is education valuable to communities and countries as well as to individuals and their families?
2. Why does Franklin think that the new generation of Americans has less ability than the founders of the colonies?

More to Life

Although settlers and colonists had their hands full carving out settlements in the wilderness, feeding and clothing themselves and their families, dealing with the Native Americans, and building social and political institutions, many like Franklin still saw the value in dedicating time to education. Additionally, people found time for more relaxing activities such as reading and writing for pleasure. Although colonists often brought literature, music, and the arts with them from their parent countries to enjoy, not all culture was imported from across the sea. New talents soon sprouted from American soil.

Phillis Wheatley, the enslaved woman represented in the image here, was the first well-known black female poet in the colonies.

7 Colonial Culture

Settlers had their hands full building and maintaining their lives and communities in the New World. However, many still found time for cultural activities. Colonists began to develop their own culture, separate from England's, through art, literature, and science. For instance, Benjamin West was a painter. He immortalized great moments in colonial history with works such as *The Death of General Wolfe* (about the French and Indian War) and *Penn's Treaty with the Indians* (about William Penn's treaty of peace with the Native Americans of Pennsylvania).

New Literature

Certain genres of books gained popularity in the New World. Books of sermons were particularly popular, as were books in which people described their own spiritual growth. Some colonists, recognizing that the settling of North

America was a historic event, wrote accounts about the founding and early years of their colonies. Examples include William Penn's *A Further Account of the Province of Pennsylvania* (1685) and Robert Beverley's *The History and Present State of Virginia* (1705).

One of the most popular forms of colonial writing was the captivity narrative. These were true stories—or mostly so—where people described being captured and held prisoner by Native Americans. *The Redeemed Captive Returning unto Zion* (1707) was a widely read example. It was written by John Williams, minister of Deerfield, Massachusetts. His whole community was killed or captured in 1704. Since these stories were supposed to show how God rescued faithful believers and returned them to civilization, Williams did not tell the complete story. His eight-year-old daughter Eunice became a member of a Native American community during her captivity. She later married a Native American man and refused to return to white society.

There were, however, a wide variety of voices in literature, as the following primary sources demonstrate.

An Enslaved Woman Finds Her Voice

Phillis Wheatley was seven or eight years old when she was kidnapped from Africa and sold into slavery in 1761. Her master and mistress allowed her to receive an education and encouraged her to become a Christian and a writer. Wheatley's poems, first published in Boston in 1770, were much admired. She was treated as something of a celebrity when she visited England in 1773.

Many of her poems were written in honor of particular events, such as funerals or journeys. In this poem, Wheatley addresses a young black painter and praises his work.

To S. M., a Young African Painter, on Seeing His Work

To show the lab'ring bosom's deep intent,
And thought in living characters to paint.
When first thy pencil did those beauties give,
And breathing figures learnt from thee to live,
How did those prospects give my soul delight,
A new creation rushing on my sight?
Still, wond'rous youth! each noble path pursue,
On deathless glories fix thine ardent view:
Still may the painter's and the poet's fire
To aid thy pencil and thy verse conspire!
And may the charms of each seraphic theme
Conduct thy footsteps to immortal fame!
High to the blissful wonders of the skies
Elate the soul, and raise thy wishful eyes.

—Reprinted in C. Herbert Renfro, ed., *Life and Works of Phillis Wheatley* (Washington, DC: Pendleton, 1916).

CONSIDER THIS

1. If Wheatley's poem is addressed to a painter and not to a poet, why do you think she speaks of "the painter's and the poet's fire" and "thy pencil and thy verse"?

The Colonies' Leading Physician Remembers His Practice

In 1745, Benjamin Rush was born into a Quaker family on a farm near Philadelphia. After studying medicine in the colonies and in Edinburgh, Scotland, he began practicing as a doctor in Philadelphia. In addition to becoming one of the most important scientists in the colonies and a leading medical teacher, Rush was a patriot. He supported America's independence from Britain and signed the Declaration of Independence. In 1800, he began writing the story of his own life for his children. In this passage, he fondly remembers his medical career serving the citizens of Philadelphia.

> From the time of my settlement in Philadelphia in 1769 'till 1775 I led a life of constant labor and self-denial. My shop was crowded with the poor in the morning and at meal times, and nearly every street and alley was visited by me every day. There are few old huts now standing in the ancient parts of the city in which I have not attended sick people. Often have I ascended the upper story of these huts by a ladder, and many hundred times have been obliged to rest my weary limbs upon the bedside of the sick (from the want of chairs) where I was sure I risqued not only taking their disease but being infected by vermin. More than once did I suffer from the latter. Nor did I hasten from these abodes of poverty. Where no other help was attainable, I have often remained in them long eno' to adminster my prescriptions, particularly bleeding and glysters, with my own hands. I review these scenes with heartfelt pleasure.
>
> —Reprinted in George W. Corner, ed., *The Autobiography of Benjamin Rush* (Princeton, NJ: Princeton University Press, 1948).

KEY TERMS AND CONCEPTS

From Phillis Wheatley's poem:
ardent Passionate.
elate the soul To make the spirit happy.
lab'ring bosom's deep intent Heart's desire.
seraphic Resembling an angelic being.

From Benjamin Rush's autobiography:
eno' Enough.
glyster Medicine given to a patient as an enema.
vermin Insects or parasites.

CONSIDER THIS

1. What reasons does Rush give for devoting so much time and energy to treating the poor?

One of the Colonies' First Woman Writers

Eighteen-year-old newlywed Anne Dudley Bradstreet came to Massachusetts with other English Puritans in 1630. Twenty years later, an English publisher issued a book of her poetry. It was called *The Tenth Muse, Lately Sprung Up in America*. According to the ancient Greeks, the Muses were nine goddesses who inspired poetry, music, art, and learning. Bradstreet's publisher was calling her the tenth Muse. Bradstreet's poems reveal her deep religious faith. They also occasionally reveal her impatience with people

This is a rendering of Anne Bradstreet's home in Massachusetts. Bradstreet was a wife and mother of eight children.

who felt that she should devote herself to "women's work," such as sewing, rather than to writing. The following passages are from her book *Meditations*. She dedicated these thoughts to her son, noting, "You once desired me to leave something for you in writing that you might look upon when you should see me no more."

> If we had no winter the spring would not be so pleasant: if we did not sometimes taste of adversity, prosperity would not be so welcome ...
>
> Youth is the time of getting, middle age of improving, and old age of spending; a negligent youth is usually attended by an ignorant middle age, and both by an empty old age. He that hath nothing to feed on but vanity and lies must needs lie down in the bed of sorrow ...
>
> All weak and diseased bodies have hourly mementos of their mortality. But the soundest of men have likewise their nightly monitor by the emblem of death, which is their sleep (for so is death often called), and not only their death, but the grave is lively represented before their eyes, by beholding their bed; the morning may mind them of the resurrection; and the sun approaching, of the appearing of the Sun of righteousness, at whose coming they shall all rise out of their beds, the long night shall fly away, and the day of eternity shall never end. Seeing these things must be, what manner of persons ought we to be, in all good conversation?
>
> —Frank Easton Hopkins, ed., *The Poems of Mrs. Anne Bradstreet (1612-1672): Together with Her Prose Remains* (The Duodecimos, 1897).

KEY TERMS AND CONCEPTS

From Anne Bradstreet's *Meditations*:

emblem Symbol.

resurrection In Christianity, the return of Christ.

CONSIDER THIS

1. How do you think Bradstreet would answer the question she asks in her final sentence?
2. Does Bradstreet believe that difficult times are important?

The Importance of Religion

Many people in colonial America were as dedicated to their faith as Bradstreet was in her writings. In fact, many came to the New World in order to dedicate themselves toward their religion away from the pressures of the church in Britain. Several of the British colonies were actually established because of religious differences. Despite the fact that some colonies were founded by those who wanted religious freedom, religion was not to be practiced freely. There were many rules and ways in which the church policed people and their beliefs. It could be said that, in some ways, religion governed the New World.

The Salem witch trials, which stretched from June 1692 to May 1693, led to nineteen people, mostly women, being hanged. Many more were imprisoned because people suspected they were witches.

8

Spirituality and Supernaturality

One of the founding principles of the United States is freedom of religion. This belief in the importance of religious freedom was part of what brought some colonists to North America in the first place. For instance, the Puritans left England in search of religious freedom.

A Break from the Church: Protestantism in America

The Church of England, Britain's national church, was established in 1534 by King Henry VIII when he wanted to break from the Catholic Church. In the later sixteenth and seventeenth centuries, however, people spoke out against what they believed to be corruption within the Church of England. The Puritans were among these people.

The Puritans began coming to the New World on the *Mayflower* with other Pilgrims. Over time, they settled the Plymouth and Massachusetts colonies, and they went to

Virginia and Maryland as well. Puritans believed they had two missions, or goals. They wanted to preach their form of Christianity to others, both Christians and non-Christians. Additionally, they wanted to continue their spiritual growth through obedience to God's word and will. Not everyone who lived in Puritan communities was a Puritan. However, ministers and church leaders had high status. The church, which came to be known as the Congregational Church, had considerable power over local affairs.

In the middle of the eighteenth century, colonial Puritans and other Protestant Christians experienced a religious revival called the Great Awakening. Led by powerful preachers and inspiring writers, this movement encouraged a return to the strict, strong faith of earlier times. Many new churches were founded in the colonies during the Great Awakening.

Other Religions in the New World

Although the majority of colonists were Protestant Christians, other religions were represented too. Roman Catholics were concentrated in some of the Mid-Atlantic states like Maryland, Delaware, and New Jersey. A few Catholics lived in Pennsylvania, although they could not vote or hold office there.

In addition to Christianity, there were a few other religions noted in the colonies. Some of the first Jews arrived in New Amsterdam in 1654. When New Amsterdam became New York, the Jewish community continued to grow. In fact, unlike Catholics in Pennsylvania, Jews could vote and hold office in New York. Small Jewish communities would develop all over the colonies. However, most were in New York, Pennsylvania, Rhode Island, South Carolina, and Georgia in the mid-1700s.

Additionally, elements of traditional African and Native American religious beliefs lingered. Unlike Jews, however, many Africans and Native Americans adopted or were forcibly converted to Christianity. This conversion was part of the mission of some

Protestants. Despite some religious diversity in the colonies, Christianity remained the ruling—literally and figuratively—religion in this land of religious freedom. Anything that stood in the way of it was seen as dangerous.

Something Wicked

In addition to religion, many people in the British colonies believed in some form of supernatural power that individuals could control. Certain people were suspected of being witches, able to use such power to harm others. The suspects were often older women, the poor, or people who challenged the existing social order in some way. Often these "witches" were seen simply as wise women who supplied a community with practical assistance in the form of herbal medicines and with harmless "magic" such as fortunetelling.

At times, however, the community took a darker view of the suspected witches, saying that they had obtained their powers from the devil. People accused of witchcraft could be punished or executed, usually with the encouragement of local religious leaders. An outbreak of accusations in Salem, Massachusetts, in 1692, led to dozens of executions. Soon, accusations and trials were under way in neighboring towns. Writes historian Frances Hill, "The witchcraft hysteria … wrecked eastern Massachusetts as would a civil war." In other words, the literal witch-hunt was as devastating as a local war might have been.

Faith on Trial

The Puritans came to Massachusetts to practice their religion freely. However, they did not believe in general religious freedom. Puritan ministers and civic leaders monitored everyone in their settlements for proper behavior such as churchgoing. They also punished anyone whose beliefs or practices did not meet their standards. These unfortunate people were fined, whipped, and

Anne Hutchinson preached from her home in Boston. Puritans did not believe that anyone other than ministers could directly receive the word from God. For that reason, Hutchinson, who was not a minister, was tried for heresy.

sometimes banished, or forced to leave the colony. For instance, the Massachusetts colony passed anti-Quaker laws in 1657 and 1658. These laws eventually led to the hanging of Mary Dyer, a Quaker woman, in 1660.

Another woman who came into conflict with the Puritan leaders was Anne Hutchinson, who was not afraid to speak her mind. Soon after Hutchinson and her husband arrived in Massachusetts from England in 1634, women began gathering in her home to pray and talk about religion. Hutchinson believed that God could speak to anyone, not just ministers. She believed people could read and interpret the Bible for themselves. This angered the Puritan ministers and leaders. In 1637, Deputy Governor John Winthrop and other leaders put Hutchinson on trial for heresy, or ideas that differ from established religious beliefs. At the end of the trial, Hutchinson and her family were banished. They moved to Rhode Island.

In this passage from the trial, Winthrop accuses Hutchinson of publicly claiming to receive the spirit or word of God directly, without the help of a minister. Hutchinson defends herself with energy and wit, which probably turned Winthrop against her all the more.

> Winthrop: You have not the right to question, you are but to answer the statement, that you made testimony, in public, that God spoke to you directly.
>
> ...
>
> Witness: Please the Court, I knew Mistress Hutchinson in Alford. One day in a churchyard she did tell me God spoke to her of the death of two children in that one year, and so it happened.
>
> Winthrop: A churchyard is a public place.
>
> Hutchinson: Sir, it is. Although there be mostly those that cannot hear.
>
> Winthrop: A public place!
>
> ...
>
> Winthrop: How do you know God revealed these things to you and not the Devil?

Hutchinson: I did not confess to either, in public. But how did Abraham know it was God's voice when He commanded him to sacrifice his only son, Isaac, and how did Abraham then know it was God's voice that stayed the knife?

Winthrop: God spoke to the prophet Abraham and so He will speak straightaway with Mistress Hutchinson: ... Remember, you are not to ask questions.

—Quoted in Deborah Crawford, *Four Women in a Violent Time* (New York: Crown, 1970).

CONSIDER THIS

1. Do you agree that the Puritans had the right to control the beliefs of those who settled in their colony?
2. Winthrop questioned whether Hutchinson voiced her religious beliefs in public. Why would that have been important to the Puritan leaders?
3. What do you imagine was the tone of Winthrop's final remark in this passage?

A Letter from One Clergyman to Another

The Mather family played a leading role in the religious and civic life of the Massachusetts colony. Richard Mather, a Puritan teacher and preacher, traveled from England to Massachusetts in 1635. His son Increase Mather was a preacher and president of Harvard College. Increase's son Cotton Mather also became a preacher. Cotton believed in supernatural occurrences. In 1689, he published a book about witchcraft and possession by evil spirits.

Some historians think he stirred up the fears that led to the Salem witch trials in the early 1690s.

The following letter is one that Cotton Mather wrote to Reverend John Cotton, his uncle and a fellow clergyman, when the trials were happening. He talks about the confessions of some accused witches. He also discusses an earthquake that destroyed the town of Port-Royal, a pirate hangout in the colony of Jamaica in the Caribbean.

Boston, Augt. 5, 1692.

Reverend Sir,—Our Good God is working of Miracles. Five Witches were Lately Executed, impudently demanding of God, a Miraculous Vindication of their Innocency. Immediately upon this, Our God Miraculously sent in Five Andover-Witches, who made a most ample, surprising, amazing Confession, of all their Villainies and declared the Five newly executed to have been of their Company; discovering many more; but all agreeing in Burroughs being their Ringleader, who, I suppose, this Day receives his Trial at Salem, whither a Vast Concourse of people is gone; my Father, this morning among the Rest. Since those, there have come in other Confessors; yea, they come in daily. About this prodigious matter my Soul has been Refreshed with some Little short of Miraculous Answers of prayer; which are not to bee written; but they comfort mee with a prospect of an hopeful Issue.

The whole Town yesterday, turned the Lecture into a Fast, kept in our meeting-house; God give a Good Return. But in the morning wee were Entertained with the horrible Tidings of the Late Earthquake at

Jamaica, on the 7th of June Last. When, on a fair Day, the sea suddenly swell'd, and the Earth shook, and broke in many places; and in a Minutes time, the Rich Town of Port-Royal, the Tyrius of the whole English America, but a very Sodom for Wickedness, was immediately swallow'd up, and the sea came Rolling over the Town. No less than seventeen hundred souls of that one Town, are missing; besides other Incredible Devastations all over the Island, where Houses are Demolished, Mountains overturned, Rocks Rent, and all manner of Destruction inflicted. The N[on] C[onformist] Minister there, scap'd wonderfully with his Life. Some of our poor N.E. people are Lost in the Ruines, and others have their Bones broke. Forty Vessels, were sunk, namely all whose Cables did not break; but no N.E. ones. Behold, an Accident speaking to all our English America.

I live in Pains, and want your prayers. Bestow them, dear Sir, on Your

C. Mather

—Cotton Mather, *Diary of Cotton Mather 1681–1724* (Boston: The Society, 1991).

CONSIDER THIS

1. Why does Mather regard the confessions of the five accused witches from Andover as a miracle?
2. Mather says the Jamaican earthquake was "speaking to all America." What do you think he imagined it was saying?

Ann Putman Confesses

In 1692, twelve-year-old Ann Putnam was one of the chief accusers in the Salem witch trials. Her fits and shrieks led to the hanging of men and women, including members of the Nurse family, her neighbors.

Fourteen years later, Putnam became a member of the congregation of Salem Village Church. She stood before the other members while the preacher read this confession to the congregation. It refers to the terrible events of the witch trials, which had come to be viewed as a terrible mistake based on false accusations. Putnam seems to have felt true regret for what she had done. Still, she placed the blame for the deaths on something outside her rather than on her own human weaknesses, which might have included confusion, jealousy, anger, or the childish thrill of becoming suddenly powerful.

> I desire to be humbled before God for that sad and humbling providence that befell my father's family in the year about '92; that I, being then in my childhood, should, by such a providence of God, be made an instrument for the accusing of several persons of a grievous crime, whereby their lives were taken away from them, whom now I have just grounds and good reason to believe they were innocent persons; and that it was a great delusion of Satan that deceived me in that sad time, whereby I justly fear I have been instrumental, with others, though ignorantly and unwittingly, to bring upon myself and this land the guilt of innocent blood; though what was said or done by me against any person I can truly and uprightly say, before God and man, I did it not out of any anger, malice, or ill-will to any person, for I

KEY TERMS AND CONCEPTS

From Cotton Mather's letter:
impudently Disrespectfully.
lecture Church service.
N.E. New England
prodigious Strange or remarkable.
rent Broken or twisted.
Sodom A city mentioned in the Bible as the home of sinful people.
Tyrius Latin for Tyre, a wealthy Mediterranean Sea port in ancient times.
vast concourse A large crowd of people.

From Ann Putnam's confession:
calamity A disastrous event.
providence Protective care of a higher spiritual power.

had no such thing against any one of them; but what I did was ignorantly, being deluded by Satan. And particularly, as I was a chief instrument of accusing Goodwife Nurse and her two sisters, I desire to lie in the dust, and to be humbled for it, in that I was a cause, with others, of so sad a calamity to them and their families; for which I desire to lie in the dust, and earnestly beg forgiveness of God, and from all those unto whom I have given just cause of sorrow and offence, whose relations were taken away or accused.

—Quoted in Frances Hill, *A Delusion of Satan: The Full Story of the Salem Witch Trials* (New York: Doubleday, 1995).

CONSIDER THIS

1. Why do you think Ann Putnam made this confession?
2. What does Putnam say was the cause of the false accusations she made?

A Minister's Warning

Jonathan Edwards was the leading religious figure of the Great Awakening. From early childhood, Edwards was trained for a career in the church. He was a teacher, pastor, and missionary. Eventually, he would be the college president of what would become Princeton University. He held Puritan ideas and beliefs and carried them into the eighteenth century.

His 1741 sermon "Sinners in the Hands of an Angry God" was meant to raise fear in the hearts of those who were not sincere in their beliefs. In Edwards's view, you didn't have to commit a crime to be a sinner—all it took was for your faith to be lazy or weak.

> O sinner! Consider the fearful Danger you are in: 'Tis a great Furnace of Wrath, a wide and bottomless Pit, full of the Fire of Wrath, that you are held over in the Hand of that God, whose Wrath is provoked and incensed as much against you as against any of the Damned in Hell: You hang by a slender Thread, with the Flames of divine Wrath flashing about it, and ready every Moment to singe it, and burn it asunder;

Jonathan Edwards was a philosopher, missionary, and theologian, or a person who studies religion. He occasionally used terror as a tactic to encourage his congregation to follow the word of God.

and you have no Interest in any Mediator, and nothing to lay hold of to save yourself, nothing to keep off the Flames of Wrath, nothing of your own, nothing that you have ever done, nothing that you can do, to induce God to spare you one Moment.

—John Smith, Harry Stout, and Kenneth Minkema, eds., *A Jonathan Edwards Reader* (New Haven, CT: Yale University Press, 2003).

CONSIDER THIS

1. According to Edwards, what is the only thing that keeps sinners from falling into hell?
2. Why do you think Edwards used so many images of fire to describe a sinner's fate?

The Question of Freedom

Although some had moved to the colonies in search of religious freedom, freedom in colonial America was policed. However, it wasn't just religious leaders policing how people should and should not live. Despite the freedom many sought, the colonies still had parents across the ocean who held all the power.

The *Pennsylvania Journal and Advertiser* published this mocking stamp—featuring a skull and crossbones, which symbolize death—in response to the Stamp Act. The act imposed a tax on all printed material in the colonies.

9 The End of an Era

Despite the fact that many people moved to the colonies in search of freedom and prosperity, the British colonies were still under British rule. Although each colony had some form of local government, the overall authority rested with governors who were appointed by the king or queen or by Parliament, the British lawmaking body.

Civil Unrest

After the middle of the eighteenth century, some people in the British colonies began to question their relationship with England. They argued that they deserved more control over their government. Some of these ideas reflected the Enlightenment, a wave of political, scientific, and philosophical thought that swept through Europe and North America.

People in America were especially influenced by the ideas of political philosopher John Locke. He wrote about what he called the "social contract." Locke claimed that individuals created governments to protect their lives, their liberty, and their property. If a government threatened those rights, it broke the social contract, which meant that the people could change or even unmake the government. American colonists started to believe they had the right to rebel against unjust rule.

Tensions Rising

After the end of the French and Indian War in 1763, various injustices frustrated the colonists. In an attempt to prevent fights with the Native Americans, Britain decided to station a large military force in the colonies. The colonists were expected to pay for this force. In some cases, they were even expected to house the soldiers. Additionally, Britain tried to please Native Americans by declaring that settlers from the colonies could not cross the Appalachian Mountains. In these ways, Americans felt that their freedom was being unfairly limited.

Matters worsened as Parliament passed a series of trade laws meant to raise money from the colonies, in part to pay the costs of the French and Indian War. Colonists reacted with surprise, frustration, and eventually anger about the new taxes and fees. They disliked having their tax money cross the Atlantic to be spent by a Parliament to which they could not elect representatives.

Over time, American opposition to the new taxes reached new heights. People refused to buy imported British goods. Women organized groups called the Daughters of Liberty to encourage the use of American-made cloth and household items. Officials who tried to enforce the new taxes were attacked. The cry "No taxation without representation!" rang out in the streets. This cry meant that colonists did not want to be taxed by a governing body to which they could not elect officials.

A Rebellion Begins

Some colonists were now talking not just of an adjustment in the colonies' relationship with Britain but of a major change. The colonists began to fall into two camps: Loyalists and patriots. Loyalists wanted to maintain the relationship with Britain. Patriots wanted to uphold their New World rights at whatever cost. Tension grew until April 1775, when fighting broke out between British troops and colonial soldiers called militiamen in Lexington and Concord, Massachusetts. Although the colonies did not declare their independence from Great Britain until more than a year later, those shots were the beginning of the American Revolution.

A Loyalist's Statement

Thomas Hutchinson, the chief judge and lieutenant governor of Massachusetts, was the second most powerful and important man in the colony in 1765. One August night, a mob burst into his house. They took everything he owned and destroyed his home. If Hutchinson and his family had not fled, the rioters might have killed them. Many people said that that attack on Hutchinson was an expression of public disapproval of the Stamp Act. This law required colonists to pay for an official stamp on printed materials. People also said that the attack demonstrated the public dislike of a colonial government that took orders from the British Parliament. But others, including Hutchinson's fellow Loyalists, called the attackers greedy gang members. Hutchinson, who later wrote a history of the American Revolution from the Loyalist point of view, made this statement the day after the riot.

> Sensible that I am innocent, that all the charges against me are false, I cannot help feeling—and though I am not obliged to give an answer to all the questions that may be put me by every lawless

person, yet I call GOD to witness (and I would not for a thousand worlds call my Maker to witness to a falsehood)—I say, I call my Master to witness that I never, in New England or Old, in Great Britain or America, neither directly nor indirectly, was aiding, assisting, or supporting, or in the least promoting or encouraging what is commonly called the Stamp Act, but on the contrary, did all in my power, and strove as much as in me lay, to prevent it. This is not declared through timidity, for I have nothing to fear. They can only take away my life, which is of little value when deprived of all its comforts, all that is dear to me, and nothing surrounding me but the most piercing distress.

I hope the eyes of the people will be opened, that they will see how easy it is for some designing, wicked men to spread false reports, raise suspicions and jealousies in the minds of the populace and enrage them against the innocent. But if guilty, this is not the way to proceed. The laws of our country are open to punish those who have offended. This destroying all peace and order of the community—all will feel its effects. And I hope all will see how easily the people may be deluded, enflamed, and carried away with madness against an innocent man.

—Quoted in Bernard Bailyn, *The Ordeal of Thomas Hutchinson* (Cambridge, MA: Harvard University Press, 1974).

CONSIDER THIS

1. How do you feel about the actions taken by the mob against Hutchinson? Even if he had supported the Stamp Act, were they justified?
2. What is the warning contained in Hutchinson's statement? Do you agree?
3. Do you think Hutchinson was persuasive in his defense? Why or why not?

John Adams Predicts the Future

One of the many colonists frustrated by the Stamp Act was Boston lawyer John Adams. His diary entries at the beginning of 1766 show that he expected the coming year to be eventful. Britain would try to enforce the Stamp Act, and Americans would resist. The clash would either lead to England punishing the colonies or recognizing their rights.

In the first of these two entries, Adams describes a letter that Mr. Deberdt, a spokesman from the colonies to the British government, had written to Lord Dartmouth, the member of Parliament responsible for the Stamp Act. In the second, he describes actions taken in various colonies against the people responsible for enforcing the act and against informers who reported violations of the act to the authorities.

In American history, Adams did far more than just write about the stirring events and issues of his time. Soon he would play an important role in the struggle for American independence.

KEY TERMS AND CONCEPTS

From Thomas Hutchinson's statement:
deluded Misled.
obliged Required.

From John Adam's diary:
abhorrence Loathing.
effigy A sculpture of someone.
equity Equal treatment.
erect To build.
gibbet Gallows, or a place from which people can be hanged.
in terrorem Latin for "to frighten them."
Jur. Jr. or Junior.
obstinate war A battle that is difficult to overcome.
race Group of people.
tempestuous Stormy.
tumult Racket or unrest.
upbraid To scold or reprimand.

We are now upon the Beginning of a Year of greater Expectation than any, that has passed before it. This Year brings Ruin or Salvation to the British Colonies. The Eyes of all America, are fixed on the B[ritish] Parliament. In short Britain and America are staring at each other.—And they will probably stare more and more for sometime.

At Home all day. Mr. Joshua Hayward Jur. dined with me. Town Politicks, the Subject. Dr. Tufts here in the Afternoon, American Politicks the Subject. Read, in the Evening a Letter from Mr. Du berdt our present Agent to Ld. Dartmouth, in which he considers three Questions. 1st. Whether in Equity or Policy America ought to refund any Part of the Expence of driving away the French in the last War? 2d. Whether it is necessary for the Defence of the B[ritish] Plantations, to keep up an Army there? 3d. Whether, in Equity, the Parliament can tax Us? Each of which he discusses like a Man of Sense, Integrity and Humanity, well informed in the Nature of his Subject ...

It is said at N. York, that private Letters inform, the great Men are exceedingly irritated at the Tumults in America, and are determined to inforce the Act. This irritable Race, however, will have good Luck to inforce it. They will find it a more obstinate War, than the Conquest of Canada and Louisiana.

January 2. Thursday. A great storm of snow last night; weather tempestuous all day. Waddled through the snow driving my cattle to water at Doctor Savil's; a fine piece of glowing exercise. Brother spent the evening here in cheerful chat.

At Philadelphia, the Heart-and-Hand Fire Company has expelled Mr. Hughes, the stamp man for that colony. The freemen of Talbot county, in Maryland, have erected a gibbet before the door of the court-house, and have hanged on it the effigies of a stamp informer in chains, in terrorem till the Stamp Act

> shall be repealed; and have resolved, unanimously, to hold in utter contempt and abhorrence every stamp officer, and every favorer of the Stamp Act, and to "have no communication with any such persons, not even to speak to him, unless to upbraid him with his baseness."
>
> So triumphant is the spirit of liberty everywhere. Such a union was never before known in America. In the wars that have been with the French and Indians a union could never be effected.
>
> —Reprinted in L.H. Butterfield, Leonard C. Faber, and Wendell D. Garrett, eds., *Diary and Autobiography of John Adams, Volume 1 1755–1770* (Cambridge, MA: Harvard University Press, 1961).

CONSIDER THIS

1. What feature of the Stamp Act uproar does Adams see as new in colonial history?
2. Do you think the colonists' treatment of those who enforced the Stamp Act was fair? Why or why not?

A Young Alexander Hamilton's Response

In the fall of 1774, the colonists created the Continental Congress. Some colonists disapproved of the Congress, calling it illegal and an insult to Britain. Samuel Seabury, a well-known priest, published pamphlets that criticized the Congress. He warned that it could plunge the colonists into a war they could not win.

Nineteen-year-old Alexander Hamilton, a brilliant student at King's College in New York (now Columbia University), replied to

Seabury in pamphlets of his own. This pamphlet was titled *A Full Vindication of the Measure of Congress.* In it, Hamilton argues that the Continental Congress has a right to exist. Hamilton presents the conflict between the colonies and Britain as a question of freedom or slavery. He recognizes that war may result. However, he believes that, in the end, the colonists will win.

Correct about colonists winning a war with Britain, Hamilton would become a US Founding Father.

> The only distinction between freedom and slavery consists in this: In the former state a man is governed by the laws to which he has given his consent, either in person or by his representative: In the latter, he is governed by the will of another. In the one case, his life and property are his own: in the other, they depend upon the pleasure of his master. It is easy to discern which of these two states is preferable. No man in his senses can hesitate to be free, rather than a slave.
>
> That Americans are entitled to freedom is incontestable on every rational principle. All men have one common original: they participate in one common nature, and consequently have one common right. No reason can be assigned why one man should exercise any power or pre-eminence over his fellow-creatures more than another; unless they have voluntarily vested him with it. Since, then, Americans have not, by any act of theirs, empowered the British

Parliament to make laws for them, it follows they can have no just authority to do it ...

It is evident that [Britain] must do something decisive. She must either listen to our complaints and restore us to a peaceful enjoyment of our violated rights, or she must exert herself to enforce her despotic claims by fire and sword ... Our numbers are very considerable; the courage of Americans has been tried and proved. Contests for liberty have ever been found the most bloody, implacable, and obstinate ... It would be a hard, if not impracticable, task to subjugate us by force.

—Reprinted in John Church Hamilton, ed., *The Worlds of Alexander Hamilton: Containing His Correspondence, and His Political and Official Writings, Exclusive of the Federalist, Civil and Military,* Volume 5 (New York: J.F. Trow Printer, 1851).

CONSIDER THIS

1. When Hamilton talks of all men having the same origin and the same right, do you think he is talking about all people? If not, why? Who might he believe unworthy of such rights?
2. What reasons does Hamilton give for America's eventual victory in a war with Britain?

The Beginning of the End

The Stamp Act led to ten years of unrest in the colonies. People everywhere talked about taxation without representation and about liberty and justice. At first, colonists simply wanted a better relationship with England. They wanted Britain to give them the rights that belonged to all British subjects or to leave them more or less alone to handle their own affairs. This was, in fact, what it had done through most of the colonial period.

However, fighting between the British and the colonists in New England in 1775 outraged King George III. This fighting made it less likely that Britain and the American colonies would be able to patch things up. Soon more and more Americans were calling for independence. None called more loudly than Thomas Paine, a soldier, thinker, and writer. In January 1776, he published a long essay called *Common Sense*. Americans bought more than five hundred thousand copies of this pamphlet. In it, Paine said that the colonists faced not a disagreement over taxes but a fight for freedom. His call for independence and unity among the "continentals" set the stage for what happened several months later, when the Continental Congress issued the Declaration of Independence. With the signing of that document, the colonial period came to an end.

> I challenge the warmest advocate for reconciliation, to shew a single advantage that this continent can reap, by being connected with Great Britain. I repeat the challenge, not a single advantage is derived. Our corn will fetch its price in any market in Europe, and our imported goods must be paid for, buy them where we will …
>
> Everything that is right or natural pleads for separation. The blood of the slain, the weeping voice of nature cries, 'TIS TIME TO PART. Even the distance at which the almighty hath placed England and America is a strong and natural proof that the authority of the one over the other was never the design of Heaven …

KEY TERMS AND CONCEPTS

From Alexander Hamilton's pamphlet:
despotic A cruel use of power.
discern To recognize.
incontestable Unable to be disputed.
preeminence Superiority.
subjugate To control by conquest.
vest To give power or rights to someone.

From Thomas Paine's *Common Sense*:
defective Faulty or desiring something necessary.
fetch To earn.
reconciliation Restoring a peaceful relationship.

But where, says some, is the King of America? I'll tell you Friend, he reigns above, and doth not make havoc of mankind like the Royal—of Britain. Yet that we may not appear to be defective even in earthly honors, let a day be solemnly set apart for proclaiming a charter; let it be brought forth placed on the divine law, the word of God; let a crown be placed thereon, by which the world may know, that so far as we approve of monarchy, that in America THE LAW IS KING ... But lest any ill use should afterwards arise, let the crown at the conclusion of the ceremony be demolished, and scattered among the people whose right it is.

—Reprinted in T.J. Stiles, ed., *Founding Fathers in Their Own Words* (New York: Perigee, 1999).

CONSIDER THIS

1. How does Paine use geography to support his call for independence?
2. What does Paine mean by "in America THE LAW IS KING"?

Declaring Independence

If Lexington and Concord marked the beginning of the American Revolution, Paine's *Common Sense* was a turning point. At last, someone had publicly voiced what people had been grumbling about since the French and Indian War: an official separation from Great Britain.

The signing of the Declaration of Independence in the summer of 1776 marked the official end to colonial America. The document, written by Thomas Jefferson and signed by prominent men like John Adams and Benjamin Rush, established that the "United Colonies" were "Free and Independent States." From these united colonies, the United States was born.

CHRONOLOGY

1607 Jamestown, the first permanent English colony in North America, is founded in Virginia.

1619 The first enslaved Africans are brought to Jamestown.

1620 Pilgrims establish the Plymouth colony in Massachusetts.

1624 The Dutch found the colony of New Netherland.

1630 The Puritan settlement of the Massachusetts Bay Colony begins.

1632 Lord Baltimore receives a grant to establish the Maryland colony.

1636 Roger Williams from Massachusetts founds a settlement at Providence in Rhode Island. Thomas Hooker from Massachusetts founds a settlement at Hartford in Connecticut.

1660 The Dutch settle in New Jersey.

1663 The Carolina colony, which later splits into North and South Carolina, is founded.

1664 An English fleet captures New Netherland, which becomes New York.

1675 King Philip's War, in which Native Americans try and fail to drive colonists out of southern New England, begins.

1676 King Philip's War ends.

1679 New Hampshire, settled by colonists from Massachusetts in the 1620s, becomes its own colony.

1681 William Penn founds the Pennsylvania colony.

1702 The New Jersey colony comes under royal control.

1704 Delaware separates from Pennsylvania to become an independent colony.

1732 James Oglethorpe establishes Georgia, the last of the thirteen colonies to be founded.

1763 The Treaty of Paris is signed, ending the French and Indian War.

1764 The British government starts to pass a series of laws and taxes meant to raise money from the American colonies. As a result, some colonists angrily begin to call for independence.

1774 The First Continental Congress meets in Philadelphia.

1775 Battles at Lexington and Concord mark the beginning of the fight for independence.

1776 The Declaration of Independence is signed.

GLOSSARY

American Revolution A war (1775–1783) primarily between Great Britain and the thirteen British colonies that would go on to form the United States.

colonial era In North America, the British colonial era lasted from 1497, when John Cabot first voyaged to present-day Canada, until the onset of the American Revolution in 1775.

colony A country or region under full or partial control of another country.

Declaration of Independence The document which formally announced that the colonies would separate from Great Britain.

export The sale of goods, crops, or material to another country.

French and Indian War A territorial war (1754–1763) that pitted the French colonists and their Native American allies against the British colonists.

frontier The land beyond the boundaries of a settled place.

Great Awakening A period of religious revival that took place in the colonies in the 1730s.

indentured servant A person who is contractually required to work for another person for a fixed amount of time, often to pay a debt.

Loyalist A person in colonial America who supported British colonial governments and the Crown.

missionary A person who works to convert others to his or her religion.

navigator A person who is skilled in plotting a course and guiding a ship or other craft.

patriot A person in colonial America who supported the colonies' independence from England.

persecute To treat someone poorly because of their religious or political beliefs.

Pilgrim Any person who left England on the *Mayflower*.

pioneer A person who explores or settles a new area, like the frontier.

primary source A document, like a newspaper article, a diary, or a book, that records a given moment or time period.

Puritan A person who believed that the Church of England needed to be reformed, or changed. Many Puritans came to North America, beginning with the voyage of the *Mayflower* in 1620. Some Puritans, known as Separatists, wanted to completely break away from the Church of England.

settlement A new place where someone founds a community.

FURTHER INFORMATION

Books

Cooper, Elaine Marie. *Fields of the Fatherless*. Raleigh, NC: Lighthouse Publishing of the Carolinas, 2013.

George, Enzo. *Colonial America*. Primary Sources in US History. New York: Cavendish Square Publishing, 2015.

Gilman, Sarah. *Colonial Jamestown*. Explore Colonial America. New York: Enslow, 2016.

Paulson, Gary. *Nightjohn*. New York: Bantam Doubleday Dell Publishing Group, 1993.

Websites

Africans in America: The Terrible Transformation (1450–1750)

http://www.pbs.org/wgbh/aia/part1/title.html

This website provides information about the lives of enslaved Africans during the colonial period.

America's Centuries

http://www.americancenturies.mass.edu/home.html

This interactive website provides many links to information and different activities related to life in the colonies.

America's Story from America's Library: Colonial America (1492–1763)
http://www.americaslibrary.gov/jb/colonial/jb_colonial_subj.html

This website provides additional primary sources related to colonial America.

Videos

The History of Colonial America
https://www.youtube.com/watch?v=Do4Ryapg3eU

This video features a musical overview of the thirteen colonies.

Plimoth Plantation: A Virtual Field Trip
https://www.youtube.com/watch?v=p5qi3Meqy24

This Scholastic video offers viewers the opportunity to look back in time and learn more about the lives of the Pilgrims and the Native Americans of the Wampanoag tribe.

Organizations

Canadian Museum of History
100 Laurier Street
Gatineau, Quebec K1A 0M8
Canada
(819) 776-7000
Website: https://www.historymuseum.ca

This museum features artifacts and manuscripts from different periods in Canadian history, including the colonial era.

La Citadelle de Québec
1 Côte de la Citadelle
Québec City, Québec G1R 3R2
Canada
(418) 694-2815
Website: http://www.lacitadelle.qc.ca/en

Built in 1693, the Citadel of Québec is the oldest military building in Canada and was the largest British fortress in the New World. This site features information about the fortress's history, like its usefulness in the War of 1812.

The Colonial Williamsburg Foundation
101 Visitor Center Drive
Williamsburg, VA 23185
(888) 965-7254
Website: https://colonialwilliamsburg.com

The foundation's mission is "to feed the human spirit by sharing America's enduring story." This hands-on museum and interactive town features colonial interpreters and ways to learn about daily life, art, culture, politics, and religion in colonial Williamsburg.

Jamestown Rediscovery: Historic Jamestowne
1368 Colonial Pkwy.
Jamestown, VA 23081
(757) 856-1250
Website: https://historicjamestowne.org

This organization offers visitors the opportunity to visit and discuss the first successful British settlement in America. Although not much remains of the original Jamestown structures like James Fort, Jamestown Rediscovery offers information about the archaeological digs happening on the grounds.

Massachusetts Historical Society
1154 Boylston Street
Boston, MA 02215
(617) 536-1608
Website: https://www.masshist.org

Founded shortly after the colonial period in 1791, this historical society and museum specializes in early American and New England–related history.

Plimoth Plantation
137 Warren Avenue
Plymouth, MA 02360
(508) 746-1622
Website: https://www.plimoth.org

Plimoth Plantation provides an interactive, interpretative experience of what it was like to live in the Plymouth colony. It highlights the lives led by both British colonists and Native Americans.

INDEX

Page numbers in **boldface** refer to images.

ABOUT THE AUTHORS

Chet'la Sebree is a writer, editor, and researcher from the Mid-Atlantic. She has received degrees in English and writing from the University of Richmond and American University. She has worked on several books about US history, including the Courting History series for Cavendish Square Publishing. Her research focus is early American history.

Rebecca Stefoff has written many books about American history, including one about the colonies and a biography of William Penn, founder of the Pennsylvania colony. Although she lives in Portland, Oregon, she used to live in Philadelphia, in the heart of a neighborhood that dates back to colonial times.